The
New Year's Eve
COMPENDIUM

The
New Year's Eve
COMPENDIUM

Toasts, Tips, Trivia,

and Tidbits for Bringing in the New Year

TODD LYON

ILLUSTRATIONS BY PATRICK MOORE

CLARKSON POTTER / PUBLISHERS

NEW YORK

Published by Clarkson N. Potter, Inc., 201 East 50th Street, New York, New York 10022.

Member of the Crown Publishing Group.

Random House, Inc. New York, Toronto, London, Sydney, Auckland

www.randomhouse.com

CLARKSON N. POTTER, POTTER, and colophon are trademarks of Clarkson N. Potter, Inc.

Printed in the United States of America

Design by Elizabeth Van Italie

Library of Congress Cataloging-in-Publication Data

Lyon, Todd.

The New Year's Eve compendium : toasts, tips, trivia, and tidbits for bringing in the New Year / Todd Lyon.

Includes index.

1. New Year.   I. Title.

GT4905.L86   1998

394.2614—dc21

98–16943

ISBN 0-609-60374-4

10 9 8 7 6 5 4 3 2

TO US

Contents

THANKS AND ACKNOWLEDGMENTS

I'm helpless without my tribe, and as usual my wonderful friends, family, and colleagues came through and poured their energy and love into this project (and me).

Katie Workman is the greatest editor a girl ever had; working with her and Erica Youngren is so much fun that I'm not sure I can even call it work. My agent, Colleen Mohyde, of the Doe Coover Agency, always makes me feel as though I'm her only client; her support, smarts, and humor continue to buoy me.

If it wasn't for the maniacal dedication of Tamara Kruchok, my research assistant and right-hand girl, this book wouldn't have been finished until, oh, 2001. Her cheerful energy saw me through many 4:00 A.M.s, as well as the occasional dawn. Thanks too to Sheilagh Mallory, who also gathered facts and evidence.

A special toast goes to Frank Vingiana, manager and wine expert at the fabulous Polo Grille & Wine Bar in New Haven, who generously shared his awesome knowledge of champagne and sparkling wine with us.

I send my blubbering gratitude to my pals who not only taste-tested the recipes in this book but also, in a few cases, actually prepared them: Lauren Caldwell, Cherie and Bob Whaples-Elliott, Tamara (again), Colleen Van Tassell, George Baker, Sue Navaretta, Sandy Shea, Steven Matzkin, Drew Cucuzza, Glenn Sasse, Jeannie Cavadini, Ben Mazzucco, Winnie and Bob Madden, and my friends at the New Haven

Athletic Club. Hugs and pats to Mamie the Love Dog, who ate all the recipes gone wrong and wagged her tail the whole time.

My family is like a multiarmed goddess, and every hand supports, guides, cajoles, and participates. Thank you, Kay, Brad, Cynthia, Barbara, Janet, Bud, Collin, Steve, Michael, Sarah, Nick, James, Trevor, and Dashiell.

For their patience, interest, and unflagging good humor I thank my coworkers at the unsinkable CT Life, with whom I've spent six great years.

Finally, I thank the magnificent, light-giving Hayward Hill Gatling, who, even in the bleakest of times, gives me a reason to wake up every afternoon.

TEN...

Where Does New Year's Eve Come From, Daddy?

*W*e know it as a night of confetti, paper hats, and sparkling wine, when every deejay's got a gig and all baby-sitters—even incompetent ones—are booked solid. It's a holiday of staying up late and priming ourselves for that crucial moment when a glittering silver ball will slowly coronate a brand-new year. In the course of ten seconds, we are collectively reborn. The old year, disguised as a withered codger, hobbles out of sight; an adorable baby in a diaper crawls in to take its place, and we all cheer with a single voice of relief and wild anticipation.

Rampant symbolism and wanton partying come together on New Year's Eve. It is our oldest holiday, and we the people continue to shape its evolution with each passing year.

ONCE A PAGAN EARTH RITUAL, NOW A TIME FOR SHINY THINGS

Long before Julius Caesar established the somewhat nonsensical Julian calendar—in fact, long before there was any such thing as a calendar—the New Year happened in early spring. Its occurrence was a natural phenomenon, dictated by the position of the sun, stars, and earth, when one growing season ended and a new one began. In virtually every ancient culture, this time of rebirth and renewal—

which we now know as the vernal equinox—was welcomed and blessed with a party.

Parties back then weren't a whole lot different than they are today. Citizens threw down their hoes, grabbed their pals and sweethearts, and ran off to eat, drink, dance, sing, and parade around in outrageous getups. These festivals of excess could last as many as eleven days and sometimes included messy rituals like rubbing the rump of a beheaded ram against temple walls (a favorite activity of high priests in Babylon).

The evening before New Year's Day was when celebrations reached their peak. This was the night that European farmers blew horns and banged on drums in order to drive off crop-destroying demons, and when Chinese party-goers banished the forces of darkness by blasting the sky with fireworks.

The official starting date of the New Year varied wildly over the centuries. From about A.D. 900 to 1200, the Italian New Year fell on Christmas Day; Japanese farmers called it January 15; the French celebrated it on Easter Sunday; and the people of the British Isles had their New Year's parties on March 25.

Our traditional January 1 celebration was established by the Roman senate long before the birth of Christ. When the Catholic Church came to power in the Middle Ages, it banished pagan rituals but slyly positioned its own religious holidays to coincide with ancient celebrations. Thus, the Feast of Christ's Circumcision allowed Catholics—as well as future Lutherans, Episcopalians, and members of various Christian orthodox sects—to celebrate the New Year alongside their heathen brethren.

NEW YEAR'S IN THE NEW WORLD

Back when the New Year was aligned with the vernal equinox, its arrival was hugely significant to people of the agricultural persuasion. In North America Iroquois tribes marked the event by aggressively driving out the old year. Dressed in disguises, men and women would go door to door and smash everything they found. Then they burned it all—grain, furniture, clothes, the whole works—in a massive bonfire. It was how they "cleaned house," making way for a brand-new year to begin.

For pious Europeans who settled in America, New Year's Eve was a night of religious observation. Many denominations held evening services, and churches pealed their bells at midnight. Nonbelievers, on the other hand, saw the holiday as a perfect opportunity for rampant rowdiness and disorderly conduct. While God-fearing citizens prayed under steeples, ruffians kept the pagan spirit alive by roaming the streets, drinking heavily, and randomly shooting guns and setting off bombs.

Over the few hundred years that followed, waves of immigrants brought their own New Year traditions to our shores. (How interesting that Ellis Island celebrates its anniversary on New Year's Day.) As a result, a whole mess of regional New Year rituals—most of which have nothing to do with organized religion—have taken root across the country. In many southern states, for instance, a dish called Hoppin' John is a traditional New Year treat. It features black-eyed peas cooked with salt pork and served over rice. The spicy concoction was first cooked up by African slaves on southern plantations, who ate it on New Year's Day in order to bring luck in the coming year.

GREAT MOMENTS IN

C. 2000 B.C.

Babylonians take up the practice of making New Year's resolutions. The two most popular resolutions are to pay off debts and return borrowed tools.

C. 600 B.C.

At festivals honoring Dionysus, god of wine and fun, Greeks ritualistically display a baby in a winnowing basket to symbolize the beginning of a new life cycle and to promise fertility in the coming year. Much, much later a baby with a banner becomes a symbol of New Year's Day.

153 B.C.

The Roman senate declares the official start of the New Year as January 1—a major switch from the traditional March 25.

46 B.C.

Julius Caesar, having inherited a messy calendar that had been repeatedly manipulated by previous emperors, has to let the year drag on for 445 days in order to make the calendar year—and New Year's celebrations—once again begin on January 1.

1886

In Pasadena, California, members of the Valley Hunt Club decorate carriages with flowers and take to the streets. The event evolves into the annual Tournament of Roses. In 1903 chariot races are added to the program; in 1916 a football game is featured. It becomes the annual Rose Bowl.

1899

Having witnessed "indiscriminate public kissing" during the 1898 New Year's celebration, San Francisco's chief of police posts extra cops on the streets to discourage necking among "persons who have not been properly presented to each other."

1976

The original First Night celebration premieres in Boston. The family-oriented event (no alcohol is served) features dozens of live performances and spectacles throughout the city and attracts about 60,000 revelers.

1985

More than 54,000 people stick kazoos in their mouths and play "A Bicycle Built for Two" in Rochester, New York. The stunt makes it into *The Guinness Book of World Records.*

1991

First Night Boston, going strong, draws a crowd of approximately 600,000. First Night New York, dwarfed even by Rochester's kazooers, draws fewer than 10,000.

1992

Czechoslovakia separates into two nations—the Czech and Slovak Republics. Slovaks have an all-night party including fireworks, bell ringing, and singing of the new national anthem. The Czech Republic has no official festivities save a solemn oath by its parliament.

NEW YEAR'S HISTORY

335

Pope Sylvester I passes away, prompting an annual commemoration, known as "Sylvester," still observed in Belgium, Germany, France, and Switzerland.

1050

In Japan the tradition of festooning one's doorway with New Year's pines, known as Kadomatsu, is firmly established. The pines act as a guide for the god of the New Year so that he may bestow good health and good luck on one's household.

1773

New Year's Eve festivities in New York City become so out of hand that laws are passed banning the exploding of firecrackers, the detonation of homemade bombs, and the random firing of shotguns.

1879

Perhaps anticipating the bright future of New Year's Eve, Thomas Edison gives his first public demonstration of incandescent lighting in Menlo Park, New Jersey.

1904

The first annual ball drop takes place in Times Square. With each passing year the ritual becomes increasingly lavish; by New Year 1998, the six-foot aluminum ball contains a fog machine, a 10,000-watt xenon lamp, 180 halogen lamps, 144 xenon glitter strobes, and 12,000 rhinestones.

1929

Guy Lombardo and his Royal Canadians perform "Auld Lang Syne" at midnight in a live radio broadcast from Times Square. Lombardo hangs on to the gig until his death in 1977.

1965

Pop psychic Criswell makes a TV appearance to announce his annual predictions. He says that Ronald Reagan will be the next governor of California. The prophecy comes true.

1973

Douglas McElvy of New York City passes away and leaves his friends $12,000 so that they may continue to drink to his memory. As of 1991, the group was still getting together in a bar each New Year's Day, ordering an extra gin and tonic for McElvy and toasting his empty bar stool.

1993

A party of four blows off its New Year's Eve reservation at a restaurant in Columbus, Ohio. The restaurant's owner subsequently sues the person who made the reservation; he seeks recompense not only for the projected cost of dinner and drinks ($60 per person) but also $200 for the private detective hired to track down the no-shows.

1994

Barbra Streisand overcomes stage fright to perform for the first time in more than 20 years at a Las Vegas concert. On the same night the Miss Howard Stern New Year's Eve Pageant grosses a reported $16 million on Pay-Per-View.

1995

The Book-Burning Society, dedicated to destroying frivolous, badly written, or boring books, holds its second annual New Year's Eve book-burning party in Colorado. An exclusive group of artists, writers, and scholars are invited to bring one copy of their least favorite book to add to the bonfire.

1996

The Hacienda Hotel in Las Vegas is demolished at midnight before a live and televised audience. Those present call the event "a blast."

For Japanese-Americans, it is not black-eyed peas but black soybeans that attract good fortune in the New Year, along with dried sardines and herring roe (caviar, anyone?). These traditional dishes were originally prepared by rice farmers in Japan to honor Toshigami, the god of the harvest.

At Philadelphia's Mummer's Day Parade, which happens every January 1, hundreds of people dress in sequins and big headdresses and march through sleet, ice, snow, and freezing rain. Though it may look like Mardi Gras with mittens, the parade has a history that reaches back to ancient Greece, when New Year dramas would be staged to symbolize the death and resurrection of crops. The custom was adopted by early British peoples, who spent New Year's Day going from house to house performing costumed plays in exchange for money and treats. The plots of these amateur productions were pretty much identical: A champion or hero would be slain in a mock fight, then resurrected by a masked doctor or high priest. Over the years, Swedes and Germans integrated similar enactments into their New Year's street festivals and parades. The resulting cultural collision was carried to the New World and became the gaudy annual spectacle in Philly.

THE WAY WE ARE

Today New Year's Eve celebrations bow to both the sacred and the secular. The holiday has evolved into a rather elegant—if indulgent—evening for grown-ups, when ladies can wear their fanciest dresses and men can turn out in their tuxes. The night is dressed in glitter and glitz; everything sparkles, from bubbles in a fluted glass to the famous orb that descends on Times Square.

Modern media have had a tremendous impact on how our celebration has shaped up—and how we share it with one another. Few people can resist turning on the TV and seeing gigantic electronic tote boards counting down to zero. We join our friends and loved ones and chant the annual countdown into cell phones, speaker phones, handsets, and headsets. We get on line and let our fingers do the cheering; we turn on the home theater system and, choosing from a hundred cable channels, fill our senses with the sights and sounds of delirious crowds from around the corner or across the globe.

Yet for all our sophisticated equipment, virtually all of us still enact ancient rites on New Year's Eve. When a woman in a thousand-dollar evening gown sticks a foil crown on her head and blows into a noisemaker, she might as well be an illiterate peasant in 1200 B.C., driving demons from her fields. In the pop of a champagne cork, we can hear the distant echo of our ancestors beating drums for luck; with our feasting and drinking, we thank the gods, as our forebears did, for another year of prosperity and abundance.

NINE

The Millennium Approacheth

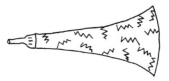

New Year's Eve has never seemed more important than it does right now. All over the world people are anticipating that magic moment when the tedious 1900s are put to rest and the new millennium comes roaring in. It's a stunning, shocking event that has happened only once before, in the year 1000, back when the feudal system dominated Europe, Vladimir I ruled Russia, Goths overtook Portugal, and clocks, compasses, pumps, and mirrors had not yet been invented.

Now that we have telephones, automobiles, and Post-It notes, everyone wants to celebrate this very significant New Year's Eve. At the stroke of midnight on December 31, 1999, we all want to be in a place we can proudly describe to our grandchildren, or romanticize in our memoirs, or keep in our private memory bank. The dawn of the millennium is an event that's bigger than a second honeymoon. It way outranks a twentieth high school reunion, or a fortieth birthday party, or a fiftieth wedding anniversary.

Which is why parties are being planned at intimate places and enchanted spots all over the globe. And it's why the planet's dance card is getting fuller every minute.

OPERATION: CELEBRATE

As early as 1984, the Millennium Society of Washington, D.C., started planning the World Millennium Charity Ball to be held simultaneously at sites in each of the world's 24 time zones, including the Great Pyramid of Cheops and the Golden Gate Bridge. The Rainbow Room in Manhattan has been booked solid for years, and so has the Ritz in Paris and the Savoy Hotel in London. By 1996 travel companies had sold out New Year's Eve packages to the Taj Mahal, the Galápagos Islands, Mount Kilimanjaro, and cruises on the Nile.

But plenty of far-flung options are still available. In South Africa a 12-hour Psychedelic Trance Concert featuring 20 live bands is planned, while in Southland, New Zealand, party-goers can descend on Bluff Hill for a laser light festival and an elaborate air show. Edinburgh, Scotland, hosts an annual Hogmanay festival that draws hundreds of thousands of revelers for five days of music and sporting events, climaxed by a torchlight parade through the city on New Year's Eve. Other parties—some massive, some medium—will take place in Machu Picchu, Istanbul, Antarctica, Sydney, and Vienna.

Times Square, which New Yorkers modestly refer to as "the Crossroads of the World," is in for a really big shindig. Its 24-hour fête will begin at 7 A.M. on December 31, 1999, when the New Year arrives in the Pacific Islands. Giant television screens will broadcast that moment and continue to carry live images from all over the world as the millennium dawns in time zone after time zone.

Seattle has appointed itself "Times Square of the West" and has made the Space Needle the central spectacle for those on Pacific Time (three hours later than New York's ball drop). Though in years past the brightly lit elevator, like a Times Square ball in reverse, rose to the top of the 550-foot structure as the countdown ensued, in 1995 pyrotechnics were added to the show, making the Space Needle the world's tallest sparkler. It's expected to burn especially bright in 1999—and so are the parties on the Needle's observation deck.

One ambitious millennialist from Florida has chartered an Air France Concorde to chase the clock and celebrate the New Year four times: first in Paris, then in Newfoundland, Vancouver, and Hawaii. As of 1997 he had a waiting list of 80 revelers ready to pay as much as $65,000 per person for the trip.

Not every celebration will be dedicated to wild times and garish spectacles. The Millennium Eve Vigil, based in Toronto, is calling upon poets and artists around the world to collectively visualize a better future. Other groups are seeking a Universal Hour of Peace starting at noon (Greenwich Mean Time) on January 1, 2000, during which every man, woman, and child on earth is invited to meditate or pray in order to "raise the consciousness of all humanity."

WHO'S CASHING IN?

For some, "ringing in the New Year" has to do with the sound of cash registers. The U.S. Patent Office has been bombarded with applications that include the number 2000 and the word *millennium*. Oodles of companies are trying to attach their slogans and logos to the turn of the millennium, but this poses a bit of a legal problem: since no one can claim ownership of the millennium, it can have no official sponsor.

Still, the event is expected to be big business for promoters, travel agents, manufacturers, tourist bureaus, countries, and major religions.

The tiny Pacific island of Kiribati, for instance, is banking on it. Kiribati will be the first place on the planet to usher in the new millennium because it adjusted the international date line back in 1995—much to the chagrin of Tonga, New Zealand, and Fiji. Kiribati officials hope its "first dawn" status will boost tourism. They need all the help they can get: in 1997 only about 4,000 people visited the island—which is about the number of visitors Hawaii gets in six hours.

In England, where the town of Greenwich plays host to Greenwich Mean Time, a dome structure described by *Newsweek* as a "giant whoopee cushion" is being erected at the intersection of the Thames River and the prime meridian. The monument will be the centerpiece of a new theme park that celebrates time itself. (Take *that*, EuroDisney.)

Pope John Paul II is a big fan of the millennium, in spite of the many prophecies that predict he'll die before it happens. His Holiness has decreed 2000 "the Great Jubilee," calling it a year of "hope and renewal." Rome is planning its own Great Jubilee celebration to tie in with the Pope's declaration.

Along with the big stuff, there's little stuff like commemorative hats, T-shirts, plates, stamps, stickers, and posters. There's also candy: M&M Mars, recognizing that M is the Roman numeral for 1,000, has launched an ad campaign with the motto, "M&Ms: Blatantly Exploiting the New Millennium."

APOCALYPSE NOW

End Time philosophers—those who believe that 2000 will mark the end of the world—expect their millennial parties to be really, really dead. Many Christians believe that the millennium is an apocalyptic event, a time when God will separate the chosen from the damned. Reverend Jim Menerfee of Atlanta, a believer that 2000 is End Time, preached in 1997 that great religious events happen in 2,000-year intervals. "The great Jewish patriarch Abraham, who established a covenant between God and man, was born in 2000 B.C. And 2,000 years later, Jesus was born. Now, as the year A.D. 2000 approaches, we're counting down to the End of Time."

Prophets, both ancient and modern, have charged the year 2000 with significance; in fact, if all the prophecies about the turn of the century came true at once, the world would be overrun by plagues, deadly meteor showers, evil fires from Hell, and perhaps even an entire polar shift. Which would mean that people partying in Tokyo would suddenly find themselves on the North Pole.

For decades, science fiction writers have created images of life after the year 2000. Their futuristic dreams have placed us in utopian societies, space colonies, and flying cars. Ancient prophets and modern psychics have had their visions, too.

• What do seers have in store for us? One ancient Buddhist manuscript predicts that by 2000, leaders in China and "the sweet land of liberty"—the land they accurately predicted would be discovered in 1492!—will agree to bore a tunnel through the Earth's core that connects the two countries. It also claims that an avalanche will bury a northern U.S. city under 40 feet of snow; a plague of incurable leprosy will develop in the Middle East and spread quickly throughout the world; and a canine-worshipping cult will liberate pet dogs and allow them to run in savage packs, "as the Great Dog God intended."

• In late 1997 eleven astrologers from five countries all predicted that on February 14, 1998, forces of darkness would rise from Hell, appearing in the East and sweeping westward. As it turns out, U.S. troops were sent to the Middle East that very week.

• According to seer Gordon-Michael Scallion, children born in 1998 will have unusual intuitive abilities and extraordinary language skills. They will also have small lungs, catlike eyes, and bluish skin.

• California psychic Mary Crane predicts that, in 2000, a woman claiming to be a goddess will attract worldwide attention.

• Astrologer Michael Lutin says that in the coming millennium the most powerful person in Hollywood will be Bette Midler.

• Reno astrologer Lynne Palmer sees a sort of mass regimentation arising in about 2008 that will require everyone to wear uniforms.

• Talk show host Conan O'Brien has his own unique picture of the future. Among other things he has announced that, in the year 2000, an angel will be born in Louisiana, sold to a carnival, and billed as "Ringhead, the Hideous Bird Boy." He also predicts that scientists will discover the secret ingredient in Starbucks coffee: a chemical that makes people forget they're paying four dollars for a cup of coffee.

• One prophecy that seems destined to come true: computers that are not programmed to recognize any number beyond 1999 as a year will experience megaglitches that could possibly echo well into the next decade. People in the medical professions are especially worried, fearing that millions of patients' records will be lost or caught in a shuffle of misdating, misfiling, and misdirection.

OUT WITH THE ONE, IN WITH THE TWO

Pythagoras claimed that "the world is built upon the power of num-
bers." Certainly our excitement about the pending millennium is built
upon that power.

Sure, there are killjoys who insist that we shouldn't bother partying at the end of 1999, because the millennium technically starts in
2001. This mathematical truth has made little difference to party-
planners, however. It's the thrill of the clicking over of the century—
like a cosmic odometer hitting 100,000—that will drive the people of
the world to make deafening noises of joy.

Think of it: For 1,000 years, the numeral 1 has dominated our lives. It has appeared at the beginning of countless four-digit sequences marking births, deaths, wars, and reigns of kings and queens and presidents; dates of Atlantic crossings made, books published, taxes returned. And as Three Dog Night will tell you, one is the loneliest number that you'll ever do. The number 2 (so much curvier and sexier than 1, don't you think?) has already hit it big on at least seven other world calendars, but one-third of living humans have been waiting all their lives for that monotonous 1 to give up its long-held post and make way for the party of 2.

When that great odometer finally clicks, we can at last celebrate the Class of O! O! O! We will be issued passports that expire in double-aught six, and children will be born who will be 12 in '12. We can look forward to anniversaries celebrated on 10/10/10, and the first person to turn 100 in 2100. Best of all, we can say that we were there, straddling two decades, two centuries, and two millennia all at once— and hollering at the moon and stars till we're dizzy with the sheer primal joy of being alive.

Your 2K Plan

*N*ew Year's Eve, for all its joyous honking and carrying-on, is also a time to ponder the major questions of life. The weightiest of these questions is: What are you gonna do?

Will you plan a trip to the moon—or someplace that seems just as far away?

Will you take a second mortgage on the house and go out for a fancy night of dining and dancing?

Will you stay close to home and hope that someone invites you somewhere good?

Or will you take the holiday by the horns and be the host with the most?

Parties are wonderful things. They reconnect us with our loved ones; they remind us that life can be full of surprises; they give us a sense of great times to come, even in bleakest winter; and they give us the perfect excuse to trot around in impossibly sexy outfits and flirt shamelessly.

Almost everybody can dress up, go to a party, and have fun; however, in order to *throw* a really good party, potential hosts and hostesses need to be blessed with certain qualities and circumstances.

HOW TO TELL IF YOU'RE A GOER OR A GIVER

DO YOU UNDERSTAND THE DEFINITION OF THE WORD *PARTY*? A party is something that is entirely outside the realm of day-to-day life. It is never "no big whoop"; you can't stick a paper hat on a predictable gathering of familiar friends and call it a party. A real party is an event designed to challenge, entertain, enchant, and liberate loved ones. It is an opportunity for humans to hyperextend their personalities, abandon their polite demeanors, and let their crazy spirits bust right out of their civilized boxes. You, as the host or hostess, must be able to set a stage upon which uptight superegos will dissolve and wild ids will be enticed to come out and play. A party is where people flirt, laugh, joke, dance, argue, act out, make out, and do things they never thought they would. It's a big responsibility, having a party, especially on New Year's Eve, and especially on *the* New Year's Eve. It requires imagination, dedication, and guts. It also requires people, a place, and a few things.

DO YOU HAVE FRIENDS? Friends are a required ingredient in every party scheme, since they usually make up the better part of a guest list. And not just any friends will do. The ideal party roster is drawn from all factions of life and includes people from all slices and strata, all of whom must have one thing in common: they must love going to parties. If you can provide such a crew, you're well on your way to having the party of the century. Or even the millennium.

A QUIET NIGHT AT HOME

THROWING A PARTY

Don't have to drive anywhere ➤	Don't have to drive anywhere
Cheap (compared to a bauble from Tiffany's) ➤	Expensive (compared to breakfast at Denny's)
Might fall asleep before midnight ➤	Might have anxiety attack before midnight
Chance to snuggle with loved ones or pets ➤	Chance to dance with loved ones and traumatize pets
Might wear nothing ➤	Might have nothing to wear
Can wear slippers ➤	Can wear 5-inch spikes
Time for meditation and reflection ➤	Time for capers, hijinks, and debauchery
Don't have to watch ball drop on TV ➤	Will be forced by guests to watch ball drop on TV
Don't have to kiss germy strangers at midnight ➤	Get to kiss everyone you've ever had a secret crush on at midnight
After midnight, might feel hollow and deprived ➤	After midnight, will probably feel bathed in love and profound satisfaction
Will likely be sound asleep by 1 A.M. ➤	Will likely be dancing a tango while being fed chocolate truffles by an incredibly attractive member of the opposite sex by 1 A.M.
At 9 A.M., will not have a hangover ➤	At 9 A.M., will not have any regrets

DO YOU HAVE SPACE? You need not dwell in a swank mansion or a posh penthouse to have a mad soirée. However, if you live in a tiny studio apartment, an unheated cabin, or your parents' basement, you should think twice about hosting a New Year's Eve party. Unless, of course, you can rent a great space.

CAN YOU AFFORD IT? It doesn't cost a fortune to throw a party—in fact, great parties can happen for very little money, as long as friends are willing to pitch in. However, there are basics that every good host/hostess needs to supply, such as mixers, ice, napkins, cups, noisemakers, decorations, a basic bar, and at least a few substantial food items. If you're not financially free enough to provide a solid party foundation, let someone else host the bash. You can do your bit by showing up with a decent bottle of bubbly and a great attitude, and offering to help clear the dirty glasses.

IS YOUR RELATIONSHIP UP TO IT? As any experienced host or hostess will tell you, party-giving is stressful. Every couple that throws a party, no matter how happy or stable their relationship might be, will have a preparty fight. It's practically guaranteed. This classic spat often begins with a simple "Darling! I thought *you* were going to borrow the extra chairs!" and escalates into vicious verbal bullets like "Your friends are all morons, and that outfit makes you look fat!" Preparty fighting is perfectly normal. However, you must honestly ask yourself: Can you and your partner get over it before the first guest arrives? Can you let the cross words evaporate, straighten your tie or touch up your lipstick, and come out smiling? If so, great. If not, the tension between you and your partner is bound to be felt by your guests and could kill everyone's party buzz.

NEW YEAR'S EVE NAYSAYERS

Some people claim to hate New Year's Eve. You may even be one of them. This negative attitude may just be random crankiness, but probably not: New Year's Eve really is a stressful holiday. For starters, it happens way too soon after the Christmas and Chanukah holidays, when everyone is still exhausted, broke, and unable to manufacture their own endorphins. New Year's Eve can seem like an unwelcome obligation, a night of forced cheer and impossible expectations that delivers more pressure than payoff.

Another problem is that New Year's Eve is the sexiest of our national holidays. Which is okay for couples, but it can send single people into the throes of self-pity. Who can blame them? At midnight, it can seem that every other person in the whole entire universe has someone special to kiss.

For seasoned party people—those who step out more than once a year and therefore don't try to cram 365 days' worth of party into one night—New Year's Eve is known as Amateur Night. Groovy scene-makers dread the annual appearance of ill-dressed citizens who attempt to experience the ultimate night out by imbibing seven different novelty cocktails before midnight and either passing out in public or weaving all over the roads.

Which leads to the worst NYE problem: driving. Yup, it's treacherous. If the drunks don't get you, the state troopers will. Every blown headlight, expired emissions sticker, and wobbly windshield wiper comes under inspection in those mandatory roadblocks. It can be difficult to loosen up and have fun when you know that, on your way home, you'll be scrutinized by flashlight and asked to hand over your license and registration. But, then, this is why God invented taxis and limousines.

It's true, there are plenty of good reasons to turn your back on New Year's Eve festivities.

But not now.

Now, all the arguments against New Year's Eve parties have lost their bite. Because this is the millennium. This is not the night to stay home and putter around the house in your plushy scuffs. When the clock strikes 2000, nobody wants to be caught running into the deli for a pack of cigs, or sitting at the kitchen table balancing the checkbook, or out back in the pen, slopping the pigs. Succumb to the pressure, the drunken amateurs, and the roadblocks, because this really is a night to remember forever.

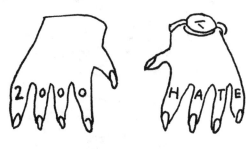

SEVEN

A Party Primer

S o, you've decided to throw a party? Good for you. Welcome to the rarefied ranks of the Makers of the Millennium.

Now, it's time to think about how you're going to ring out the old and bring in the new. There are about 2,000 options. You could invite your friends to pack their tents, camp out in a valley, dance by torchlight, and toast the stars in a wide-open sky. You could charter a boat and float into the New Year like a tiny republic populated by your favorite people. You might rent a hall and hire a killer band, or get an off-season lease on a summer camp with a dozen cabins where dogs and children are welcome, or host a seven-course sit-down dinner, or reserve a Pullman on a vintage train.

But there's no guarantee that any of these creative soirées would be any more fun than a cocktail party held in your own home. After all, where you live is where you love, and where you love is where you celebrate. Worried that a home-based party won't meet hopped-up millennial expectations? Read on.

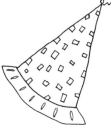

THE HOPES AND FEARS OF ALL THE NEW YEARS: AUNTIE MAME VERSUS MARY TYLER MOORE

In all of literature and film, there was never a better party-giver than Auntie Mame. Rent the Rosalind Russell version and see for yourself: Mame is introduced in the middle of a party in the midst of Prohibition, and the soirée is a masterpiece. There's exotic decor, specialty drinks, fascinating food, and mobs of people—including a trio of drag kings—who seem to hail from every corner of the globe. Everybody is talking and laughing and carrying on in a gleeful crush of colorful humanity.

Some 20 years after that movie was made, popular culture gave us another memorable hostess: Mary Richards, as played by Mary Tyler Moore.

You remember Mary Tyler Moore, don't you? She played the sunny gal from Minneapolis who could turn the world on with a smile. She called her boss "Mr. Grant," her favorite kind of pizza was plain, and she hosted such painfully boring and awkward parties that today any sparsely attended gathering marked by long silences, self-conscious throat-clearing, and polite excuses to leave early is known as a Mary Tyler Moore Party.

There's a tiny Mary Tyler Moore living inside all of us. She walks the floors of our minds in modest platform shoes and is always on the verge of tears. "What if my party is dreadfully dull?" asks our inner MTM. "What if my guests have nothing to say to each other? What if *no one shows up*?" Though Prozac has been known to take the hysterical edge off her voice, the best way to silence our inner Mary is to make a party that's bomb-proof. And that takes a little bit of knowledge, a lot of planning, and an unshakable faith that the spirit of Auntie Mame will pull us through.

THE FUNDAMENTAL PRINCIPLES OF PARTY-GIVING

When you were seven years old, parties were great. You'd be dropped off on a Saturday afternoon in your best dress-up clothes with a big package under your arm, all excited about giving a present yet secretly jealous that the present wasn't for you.

Everybody got to the party at the same time (you knew it was the right place because there were streamers and balloons everywhere). And right away the games began. There was Musical Chairs and Pin the Tail on the Donkey, contests involving blindfolds and balloons, prizes for winners, and if the party was fancy, maybe a clown, a magician, or pony rides. Each activity led into the next beautifully, all perfectly coordinated by a mystical force we now know as the adult. When it was time for cake, the kids scrambled to find their places at a decorated table, where hats and noisemakers and loot bags were laid out just for them. Everybody sang "Happy Birthday to You," and everyone left at exactly the same time.

Here's what didn't happen at parties when you were seven: You weren't expected to stand around and make small talk. Everyone in your class and/or neighborhood was there, and everyone joined in the games. There was never nothing to do, and the party never dragged on for too long.

This is why seven-year-olds don't dread parties.

And this is why, if you take a tip from kiddie parties, nobody will dread your gatherings, either. Here are some adult-size strategies:

- Don't plan a low-key little affair—this is no time for holding back. Besides, people have their own version of the low-key little affair every night in the privacy of their own homes, and it usually involves a remote control, a bag of chips, and comfortable footwear.

- Make sure your party has a beginning, a middle, and an end. Clearly state the agenda on the invitation. (Example: "party from 9 P.M. to 2 A.M.; fortunes told from 10 to midnight.") Gently enforce end time with polite comments such as "Oops! It's two A.M. and I'm about to turn into a pumpkin!" Unless, of course, the party's so swinging that you can't bear to break it up.

- Decorate like crazy.

- Organize activities, including games, contests, spectacles, and surprises that engage every guest.

- If you can afford it, include professional entertainment.

- Dress up. As the host or hostess, it's your job to be the fanciest person there, so that none of your guests will feel overdressed. (Remember how the birthday girl always wore the biggest, fluffiest party dress? That's you.)

- Invite too many people. Professional party boy P. J. O'Rourke has a formula for determining the size of your guest list: Figure out how many people your home will comfortably hold, and invite ten times that many people. His calculations might be a little extreme, but it's much more fun to be crushed by party-goers than to wander through rooms populated by brimming bowls of chips, tumbleweed, and crickets.

- Provide an abundance of good food and good drink, and keep it coming.

- Don't wait on your guests. Offer a first drink, pass trays of hors d'oeuvres if you've got them, then leave them alone. Most of the mingling that goes on at parties happens at the bar and in the buffet line; people want to fetch their own food, drinks, and Extra-Strength Excedrin so they can move around and check out the demographics.

- Don't worry too much about seating. At parties, most people choose to stand.

- Establish good flow. Never line chairs up against walls; seating areas should be clustered in the center of rooms, forcing movement to happen along the outskirts.

- Have good ventilation and cool temperatures. Borrow as many fans as you can, and run them all night long.

- Try not to segregate smokers unless there's a genuine asthma problem to cope with. If necessary, set up a separate smoking room, deck, or porch, and supply these areas with plenty of ashtrays. A better solution, if possible, is to set up a smoke-free zone where nonsmokers can escape to, if they choose.

- Gracefully endure spills on the carpets, crumbs in the sofa, rings on the coffee table, and an occasional broken glass or plate. Anything very precious or fragile should be put away.

- Be prepared to have a few unscheduled overnight guests. Whether it's due to inebriation, exhaustion, infatuation, or car trouble, one of the hallmarks of a great party is that there are still people there the next day.

WHO WILL COME TO YOUR PARTY?

Many otherwise brilliant hosts and hostesses make a crucial error when planning their guest list: they invite only members of their own tribe. This, while cozy and comfortable, practically guarantees a room full of people who dress alike, talk alike, and already know each other's jokes. The result is a party that's homogenized at best and, at worst, dull.

Creating a great guest list is a lot like making soup. You need to start out with plenty of stock (a stable of good friends, preferably charming, rich, and attractive). To this base you add a variety of ingredients that range from the benign (cheerful coworkers) to the daring (your unemployed neighbor who spends all his time at poetry slams). (Note: Although unstable ex-lovers, vengeful employees, and dull relatives might add volume to your party, these are not quality ingredients and should be avoided. But do invite any person of any age, shape, or size who makes you laugh.)

In soup, as in life, the most delicious mixes balance yin against yang. If you're going to invite an art history professor, also invite a wisecracking hairdresser. Put an astrophysicist on your list, and add a bodybuilder for contrast. Throw the potters in with the financial planners; mix the bikers with the environmentalists.

And if you really want to add spice, flavor your party with wild-card guests like a cross-dressing sushi chef, a rodeo star, a dominatrix, and a blues guitarist. Don't worry if you barely know these people—invite them anyway. When wild-card candidates show up, it's great. When they don't, nobody notices.

INVITATIONS, PLEASE

It's never too early to send out invitations to a millennium party. In fact, you should be sending them out right this minute. If you're not sure how your party is going to look, or where it will be held, or at what time it might take place, you should at least send out "save the date" cards. Then, as the event draws closer, you can mail proper invites with all the details. Don't expect a flood of RSVPs, however. Thirty percent of Americans—and even more in the Northeast—confess to ignoring their RSVP duties. Take this into account when you're trying to gauge how many people will show up.

SIX

What's Your Theme?

*B*ack in 1963 James Beard wrote rapturously about the American cocktail party, calling it the "twentieth-century salon." He praised its "spirit of relaxed gaiety" and its quality of being "as democratic as the subway."

The cocktail party, with its surefire mix of food, libations, music, and conversation, make it the ideal model for the ultimate New Year's Eve party. But in these giddy premillennial days, the cocktail party begs to be gussied up, tricked out, and otherwise elevated into the realm of the fantastic. That's where theme parties come in.

Great theme parties have a focus, a slant, a style all their own. They set a thrilling stage upon which guests can unleash wit and wild behavior. The boldest party-goers will rise to the challenge of a theme party in high style and bring much more than conversation and a bottle of wine to the table. Even the shy and the bashful, who aren't apt to dress up or role-play, will enjoy the show.

Following are but a few concepts that can be spun into enchanted evenings.

THE SPACE-AGE BACHELOR PAD PARTY

Everybody has an inner lounge lizard; here's the chance to get in touch with yours. Ask your guests to wear slick outfits from the swingin' sixties—think sharkskin suits, butt-hugging cocktail dresses, bouffant 'dos, spike-heeled shoes—and serve retro cocktails like the Pink Squirrel, the Zombie, and the Oh, Nurse. Lush lounge music, peppered with cha-chas and twists, will inspire party-goers to swing their fringe and call one another "doll" and "daddy." *Brave* hostesses can wear Playboy bunny costumes; brave hosts can dress like Hef, complete with pipe and satin smoking jacket. By the end of the evening, every man will think he's Peter Gunn and every woman will think she's Tuesday Weld.

- **DECORATIONS:** Colored lightbulbs in all lamps; plastic palm trees; cocktail napkins with kooky slogans; fishnets slung from the ceiling; faux leopard cushions for lounging; tiki torches; Aqua Net and Hai Karate in the bathroom.
- **FOOD:** Cocktail weenies; Polynesian shrimp; Swedish meatballs; Chex party mix; Ritz cracker canapés; fondue; Allsorts; bridge mix.
- **DRINK:** A basic bar, plus sparkling wine; at least one house cocktail (Grasshopper, Singapore Sling, Pink Lady, Stinger); Tab in cans; Tang.
- **MUSIC:** Mancini; Bacharach; Esquivel; anything from Capitol's Ultra Lounge series.
- **GAMES:** Twister, Pass the Orange, Spin the Bottle.
- **ADDED ATTRACTIONS:** A limbo contest.

- **WHAT TO DO AT MIDNIGHT:** Go heavy on the horns, hats, confetti, and kissing. Ideally, a Tom Jones impersonator should sing "Auld Lang Syne," then segue into "It's Not Unusual."
- **SOUVENIRS:** Printed matchbooks and swizzle sticks.

2 CRUISE INTO 2000

All those procrastinators who tried and failed to book a millennial cruise will appreciate this party. It's a lavish, high-budget affair that re-creates New Year's Eve on a grand ocean liner, complete with elegant surroundings, sumptuous spreads of glorious food, and lots of good champagne. Guests can dress their very best—gowns and tuxedos are appropriate—and be prepared to dance, feast, and gamble. You, as captain of the ship, will have nothing to do but mingle and enjoy yourself, since you will be surrounded by caterers, servers, florists, and dance escorts hired for the event.

- **DECORATIONS:** Massive flower arrangements; stars projected all over the walls, ceiling, and floor of the dance area; nautical touches.
- **FOOD:** Passed hors d'oeuvres, a raw bar, a fabulous buffet, and a breakfast spread after midnight.
- **DRINK:** A full bar and endless supplies of bubbly.
- **MUSIC:** A live band or orchestra specializing in swing, jazz standards, or classic soul.
- **GAMES:** Blackjack and baccarat in the casino room with a professional dealer.
- **ADDED ATTRACTIONS:** A photo booth where guests can

have New Year's Eve portraits taken against an ocean liner backdrop (helm required).

- **WHAT TO DO AT MIDNIGHT:** Pass around half-masks, paper poppers, and confetti; deliver a champagne toast; then let the band count down to ecstasy.
- **SOUVENIRS:** Cigars with commemorative bands; tiny vials of perfume with special issue labels.

3 THE DANCE OF THE DO-GOODERS

This is a party with heart: its object is to raise money for charity or for a friend in need. Guests are asked, well in advance, to contribute something to be bid on in a silent auction. This can be an object (artists can donate a painting), or a professional service (dentists can offer a free filling), or a not-so-professional service (a weekend of pet-sitting). It can also be something absurd, like an offer to mow the highest bidder's lawn dressed only in BVDs. Close the bidding at 11:30 or so and then announce the winners right after midnight.

- **DECORATIONS:** Classic gala stuff, like flowers, balloons, spangles, and sparkles, plus a prominent table with a display of items up for auction and a slotted box next to each. Guests write down their bids and slip them in the box.
- **FOOD:** Hors d'oeuvres and a spread to nibble on all night; coffee and pastries after midnight.
- **DRINK:** A basic bar, plus sparkling wine and a house punch (see Chapter 5).

- **MUSIC:** Taped or live music conducive to dancing and carrying on.

- **ADDED ATTRACTIONS:** A kissing booth to raise extra donations, operated by eager volunteers. Note: Donations are highest if you ask patrons to pay up *after* the kiss, and to have their contribution reflect their level of kissing satisfaction.

- **WHAT TO DO AT MIDNIGHT:** Count down, throw streamers and confetti, sing, make a toast. Then, with all your guests assembled, announce the results of the auction. At some point later in the evening, when all the calculations are done, call everyone together again to announce the total dollar amount raised. This is a perfect opportunity to make another toast and applaud your friends for their generosity.

- **SOUVENIRS:** Wax lips (handed out at the kissing booth).

THE PAJAMA BALL

Many, many people spend the better part of November and December squeezing into stylish black clothing and fake-smiling at obligatory holiday events. For them, the Pajama Ball is a godsend. Guests are encouraged to wear pajamas, or some version of loungewear; if your friends are creative, they'll show up in curlers, shower caps, kimonos, union suits, lingerie, Dr. Denton's, smoking jackets, and bunny slippers, and sprawl all over the place like teenagers at a sleep-over. This party proves that you don't have to hold your stomach in or endure painful footwear to have fun.

- **DECORATIONS:** Pillows and cushions on the floor; novelty sleeping bags to be rolled out at will; a game room with cards, dice, and board games.

• **FOOD:** Pizza, finger sandwiches, popcorn balls, cheese puffs, s'mores.

• **DRINK:** A basic bar, sparkling wine, and hot chocolate with or without Kahlua.

• **MUSIC:** Soul and R&B hits from the 1970s.

• **GAMES:** Charades, Truth or Dare, Killer, Concussion, Poker, Bingo.

• **ADDED ATTRACTIONS:** A psychic, astrologer, or palmist to give readings, or a gaggle of beauty operators to give manicures, pedicures, and/or facials.

• **WHAT TO DO AT MIDNIGHT:** Watch the ball drop on TV; at the big moment, have your guests beat the hell out of a huge piñata filled with treats and treasures.

• **SOUVENIRS:** Printed toothbrushes.

5 THE YEAR OF LIVING DANGEROUSLY

Some years are so packed with dramatic events and sudden twists in the road of life that, by December, you and everyone you know has got whiplash. If 1998 or 1999 fits this description, then the Year of Living Dangerously is the party for you. It begins with an invitation that asks guests to list all the memorable things that happened to them that year (for example: audited by the IRS, dated Cher, vacationed in New Jersey, purchased "handyman's special" in mudslide zone). The questionnaire is returned as an RSVP, and it is upon these personal accountings that the party is based.

• **DECORATIONS:** Beautiful setups punctuated with incongruous objects like tires, police barricades, skeletons in closets, and feet protruding from under sofas. Note: This party requires either a working fireplace or an outdoor bonfire. A Weber grill or hibachi will also do in a pinch.

• **FOOD:** Yummy stuff with the odd horror mixed in: a rubber finger on the cheese tray, for example, or handcuffs locked around the salami, or any snacks or libations featured in Penn and Teller's *How to Play with Your Food*.

• **DRINK:** See above. You might want to float an eyeball in the punchbowl, or slip a few subpoenas in with the cocktail napkins.

• **MUSIC:** A mix of your favorite tunes, along with a few of your least favorite tunes.

• **MAIN ATTRACTION:** At about 11 P.M., the host or hostess reviews the most dramatic questionnaires, reading choice tidbits aloud. Then the winner—that is, the person who has had the most tumultuous 12 months—is crowned Ms. or Mr. Dangerous and receives gifts, a trophy, an ermine cape, whatever. The rest of the questionnaires are gathered up and brought to the fireplace or outside to a bonfire, where they are ceremoniously burned to a crisp at the stroke of midnight.

FIVE

Eat, Drink, and Be Daring

*O*ptions for party menus are so vast that they could make a party-giver dizzy. At the top of the party food chain are dazzling tableaux dripping with oysters, caviar, and rare roast beef; at the bottom are TV trays piled with bags of chips and cans of squirt cheese.

Somewhere in between gourmet and bargain basement fare is the classic cocktail party spread. This all-night feeding station is usually presented as a table laden with cheeses, pâtés, olives, breads, crackers, vegetables, and fruits that remain in place all night and are periodically refreshed. The cocktail party spread is a host/hostess's best friend, because it can be set up in advance and requires very little maintenance.

Every seasoned party-giver has his or her favorite version of the cocktail party spread. Some emphasize meatless offerings; others periodically add hot foods, fresh from the oven. There are hosts who splurge on smoked salmon with all the fixings; still others insist that a spiral-cut ham, presented with crusty bread and an assortment of mustards, is always their biggest hit—even though half their friends claim to be "almost vegetarian."

Whatever variations you may choose, it helps to start with the basics. A standard, all-purpose party spread should include two soft cheeses and two hard cheeses; one vegetarian pâté; one goose or chicken liver pâté; one dish of oil-cured black olives; a platter of crudités with a crowd-pleasing dip; grapes and berries, for garnish as well as for nibbling; hummus; a spreadable cheese; an herbed salami; four varieties of crusty bread; and at least three baskets of crackers. Foods should be arranged in a variety of vessels on a large cloth-covered table that's easy for guests to reach. Include stacks of plates, plenty of napkins, and forks, if appropriate, plus decent lighting so that guests can clearly see what they're reaching for.

Once your "anchor" foods are in place, you are free to treat everyone to a parade of clever canapés and amusing hors d'oeuvres, passed on trays or placed strategically between clusters of revelers. Serve these special bites within the first hour or so of your party, and let guests continuously help themselves to cheeses and nibbles at the table. Close to midnight, when champagne flows like a twinkling river, set out sweets for your guests to enjoy. Plates of chocolate truffles, delicate party cookies, and miniature fruited tarts are all good choices. Much later in the evening (or early in the morning, rather) you may want to set out another round of trays laden with pastries and coffee.

Following are some simple party-starters that look lovely, taste divine, and are easy to eat with one hand. A note about quantities: The average guest can consume as many as eight hors d'oeuvres or canapés over the course of two hours. A simple formula is to prepare four varieties (or at least one vegetarian and one without seafood) and make enough so that each guest can have two of each kind.

SALMON CANAPÉS JAPONAIS

(MAKES 24)

The ingredients can be prepared up to 6 hours in advance and stored, covered with plastic, in the refrigerator. Don't assemble until immediately before serving.

8 ounces smoked salmon, thinly sliced
Table water crackers
Prepared wasabi
1 daikon radish, sliced paper-thin
Chives, snipped into 1-inch lengths

1. Lay a slice of salmon on each cracker.
2. Smear a dollop of wasabi on each radish slice, and place (wasabi side down) on top of salmon.
3. Garnish with the chives.

MACADAMIA CHICKEN FINGERS

(MAKES 20)

2 cups all-purpose flour
2 teaspoons salt
12 ounces unsalted macadamia nuts, finely chopped
4 eggs
½ cup butter, melted
1 pound skinless, boneless chicken breast, cut into about 20 finger-size strips

1. Preheat oven to 350°F.
2. Mix flour with salt in a plastic bag with a sealable top; pour chopped macadamias into another. Place the eggs in a shallow bowl and beat

lightly. Pour the melted butter into a small bowl.

3. Dip chicken strips in melted butter, then place in flour-filled bag and shake to coat. Remove and shake off excess flour.
4. Dip strips in egg mixture, then drop in nut-filled bag and shake to coat.
5. Bake on nonstick cookie sheet for approximately 20 minutes.

SHRIMP SEVICHE

(MAKES APPROXIMATELY 24)

2 pounds jumbo shrimp, cooked and peeled
½ cup fresh lime juice
¼ cup olive oil
4 scallions, trimmed and minced
2 fresh jalapeño peppers, minced
½ cup fresh chopped cilantro
1 teaspoon freshly ground black pepper
1 teaspoon kosher salt

1. Combine the shrimp, lime juice, oil, scallions, jalapeño peppers, cilantro, black pepper, and salt in a large glass bowl.
2. Cover tightly and refrigerate for at least 2 hours and up to 12.
3. To serve, spear each shrimp with a long, slender wooden skewer.

BOMBAY EGGS

(MAKES 24)

12 hard-boiled eggs
1 tablespoon butter
1 small onion, finely chopped
5 tablespoons mayonnaise
2 tablespoons prepared mango chutney

4 teaspoons high-quality curry powder or paste
Salt to taste
Paprika

1. Peel the eggs; slice in half lengthwise; remove yolks and reserve.
2. In a small pan, melt the butter and sauté the chopped onion over medium heat until translucent, about 5 minutes.
3. With a spoon or in a mixer, combine the egg yolks, the onion, mayonnaise, chutney, curry powder, and salt, and mix until smooth.
4. Spoon the yolk mixture back into the hollows of the egg whites (or pipe with a pastry bag with a wide tip for fancier presentation) and sprinkle with paprika.

SAVORY PARTY TARTS

(MAKES 24)

2 tablespoons butter
2 medium leeks, white and light green parts only, trimmed and coarsely chopped
4 ounces cheddar cheese, shredded
2 egg yolks
½ cup heavy or whipping cream
1 teaspoon Dijon mustard
1 teaspoon Worcestershire sauce
Salt and freshly ground black pepper to taste
24 preprepared mini pastry shells (phyllo or other)
Pimentos or sweet roasted peppers, cut into strips

1. In a skillet over medium heat, melt the butter. Sauté the chopped leeks until tender, about 7 minutes. Allow to cool.
2. In a large bowl, combine the cheese, egg yolks, cream, mustard, Worcestershire, leeks, salt, and pepper. The consistency should be creamy; add extra cream if needed.

3. Spoon the mixture into pastry shells, and top each with a slim strip of roasted red pepper.
4. Bake according to pastry shell instructions. Serve warm or at room temperature.

NOTE: This recipe can be made up to two days in advance, refrigerated (not frozen), and warmed before serving.

SPARKLING CAVIAR DIP
(MAKES 1 CUP—SERVES 24)

8 ounces whipped cream cheese, at room temperature
2 tablespoons sour cream
1 tablespoon chopped chives
1 tablespoon chopped scallions
4 ounces salmon roe caviar (salmon roe, flying fish roe, or red lumpfish)
2 cucumbers, sliced but not peeled

1. Beat the cream cheese and sour cream together.
2. Stir in the chives and scallions.
3. Transfer into a serving bowl and chill, covered, until ready to use.
4. When ready to serve, drain the caviar on paper towels, and then gently fold into the cream cheese–sour cream mixture.
5. Serve immediately with cucumber slices. You can make the cream cheese–sour cream mixture 4 hours in advance and store, covered, in the refrigerator.

CRISPY GOAT KISSES

(MAKES 30 KISSES)

2 sheets phyllo dough
4 tablespoons butter, melted
4 ounces chèvre (goat cheese)
2 tablespoons fresh sage, chopped

1. Preheat oven to 350°F.
2. Place one phyllo sheet on a flat surface and brush with melted butter. Place the second sheet of phyllo over the first, and brush with butter.
3. Cut the phyllo into 30 squares.
4. Place a dollop of chèvre in the center of each square and add a tiny sprinkling of sage.
5. Pull the corners of each square over the cheese and twist to form a kiss.
6. Bake for about 10 minutes, or until lightly browned.

THE BAR IS OPEN

It's not necessary to set up a full bar when entertaining at home—even if you're throwing what's technically known as a cocktail party. A modified bar that includes beer, wine, champagne, sodas, mixers, and a few select cocktail fixings is perfectly appropriate, even for big wing-dings.

When calculating how many bottles to buy, remember that the average party-goer has one drink per hour—two, when it comes to champagne—and that there are five to six drinks in a standard-size bottle of wine or champagne. This time-honored formula takes non-drinkers, light drinkers, and heavy drinkers into account; therefore you should include the total number of your anticipated guests when deciding how much alcohol to buy.

Note: Never underestimate how much ice you'll need. Count on going through a half-pound of ice per person—not including all the ice you'll need for coolers and champagne buckets.

About two hours before your party begins, you should have the bar completely set up. Bottles of beer, soda, champagne, and white wine should be set in great vats of ice to cool; glassware should be assembled; liquors and mixers should be set in place. And napkins should be nearby in case there's a spill.

OUR FRIEND GLASSWARE

In a perfect world all hosts and hostesses would have fleets of gleaming glasses at their disposal. They'd never run out of snifters, pilsners, flutes, cordials, or martini glasses. For every Manhattan they'd have a maraschino cherry, and for every Gibson they'd have a sly cocktail onion and a witty pick to stab it with.

Unfortunately, most of us have to factor in that boring variable known as reality.

It's okay: no one can be reasonably expected to have more than a dozen of any one style of glass in his or her breakfront. Luckily, party rental houses and catering companies know this. They are more than happy to rent all kinds of glassware for any event. You can choose

goblets, rocks glasses, Tom Collinses, and sours; you can stock your party with tulips, white wine glasses, red wine glasses, ponies, and shot glasses.

Or, if you're a good shopper, you can buy bargain glassware that's so cheap, it's almost disposable. Many odd-lot stores, flea markets, and restaurant supply companies stock cases of very inexpensive glasses that may not be adorable but will definitely lend a certain cachet to an otherwise low-budget event.

If you must choose only one style of glass with which to service your whole party, it's smart to go for goblet or balloon glasses. These can range in size from a modest 6 ounces to a whopping 10. Choose the largest you can find, in order to accommodate virtually all drinks, including cocktails, beer, wine, and cognac.

When budgets are truly squeezed, plastic cups may be the order of the day. If such is your situation, buy two sizes: large, 8-ounce cups for beer and sodas; and smaller cups, about 6 ounces each, for wine and cocktails.

How many glasses should you have on hand? That's easy: Whether you're arranging a stunning assemblage of drink-specific crystal or scrounging paper cups with Teenage Mutant Ninja Turtle motifs, you should always supply a minimum of three drinking vessels per guest.

Important note: If sparkling wine is to be served, try to make room in the budget for champagne flutes (again, these can be rented for the occasion). If such a solution is out of reach, the second-best choice is small clear cups of the 4-ounce (or so) persuasion. Though plastic "champagne glasses" can be readily purchased at party stores, these should be avoided. Why? Because most of them have a fatal (literally) design flaw. That is, they're assembled from two interlocking parts: the flat base and the curvy stem/saucer portion. The base, because it isn't glued to the stem, tends to fall right off. Which means that guests end up walking around with a lethal stabber of bubbly that can't be put down (except, perhaps, in houseplants or hunks of cheese). This prohibits desirable party behavior like dancing and gesturing wildly while flirting, and can lead to spillage and injuries.

TOOLS OF THE TRADE

When setting up a party bar, certain bartending equipment comes into play. As with glassware, there are high-end solutions that anticipate the wishes of every persnickety guest that might walk through the door. There is also a list of rock-bottom essentials. We'll start with that.

THE DRINK OF THE HOUSE

One festive addition to any party bar is a "signature" cocktail, that is, a specialty of the house that's yours alone. The best signature cocktails are short, not too sweet, served in an attractive glass, and offered to your guests at the very beginning of the evening. You can (and should) lift the recipe for your signature cocktail from a bartending book—or this book—but do give your house cocktail an intriguing name of your own invention.

Following are some cocktails up for adoption.

BASIC BAR SETUP

- Corkscrew
- Bottle opener (aka church key)
- Ice bucket and tongs
- Stirrer
- Sparkling wine
- Beer (preferably bottled)
- White wines (dry varieties from France, Spain, California, Chile, or Australia are good choices)
- Red wines (merlots, cabernet sauvignons, zinfandels, or syrahs from virtually any country are recommended)
- Vodka
- Scotch
- Cola
- Diet cola
- Tonic
- Orange juice
- Cranberry juice
- Club soda
- Spring water
- Lime slices
- Lemon slices

FANCIER SETUP

All of the basic bar setup, plus:
- Cocktail shaker
- Strainer
- Jigger
- Light rum
- White tequila
- Bourbon
- Gin
- Lemon twists
- Green olives
- Maraschino cherries
- Grapefruit juice
- Tomato juice
- Lemon/lime soda

FULL BAR

All of the basic and fancier setups, plus:
- Muddler
- Electric blender
- Bar spoon
- Measuring spoons
- Martini pitcher
- Champagne stopper
- Brandy
- Cognac
- Triple Sec
- Kahlua
- Single-malt whiskeys
- Grappa
- Gold tequila
- Aquavit
- Sambuca
- Campari
- Curaçao (white and blue)
- Dubonnet rouge
- Port
- Pernod
- Dry sherry
- Dry vermouth
- Sweet vermouth
- Angostura bitters
- Rose's Lime Juice
- Milk or cream
- Sugar cubes
- Sugar syrup
- Tabasco sauce
- Grenadine
- Cocktail onions
- Orange slices
- Celery
- Horseradish
- Margarita salt
- Seltzer (with a siphon)
- Pineapple juice

Soul Kiss

(MAKES 4)

4 jiggers bourbon
2 jiggers dry vermouth
2 jiggers Dubonnet rouge
2 jiggers orange juice
Orange peel, for garnish

1. Combine the liquid ingredients over ice in a cocktail shaker.
2. Stir and strain into chilled martini glasses.
3. Garnish with orange peel.

Hot and Icy

1 small habañero (Scotch Bonnet) pepper
1 liter vodka
½ lemon

1. Using great care and protecting yourself with latex gloves, quarter the habañero pepper, remove and discard the seeds, and add the pepper pieces directly into the bottle of vodka.
2. Cut the lemon into small pieces and add.
3. Place the bottle in the freezer at least 2 hours but no more than 4 hours before serving.
4. Strain and serve the vodka over ice, with festive swizzle sticks as "garnish."

NIGHT OF THE IGUANA

(SERVES 4)

4 jiggers vodka
2 jiggers Triple Sec
2 jiggers limeade
1 jigger fresh lime juice
Lime slices, for garnish

1. Combine the liquid ingredients over ice in a cocktail shaker.
2. Stir and strain into chilled cocktail glasses.
3. Garnish with the lime slices.

NEGRONI

4 parts gin or vodka
2 parts Campari
1 part sweet vermouth
Orange twist, for garnish

1. Combine the liquid ingredients over ice in a cocktail shaker.
2. Shake and strain into a chilled cocktail glass.
3. Garnish with the orange twist.

Fair and Warmer

4 parts light rum
1 part sweet vermouth
3 dashes white curaçao
Lemon twist, for garnish

1. Combine the liquid ingredients over ice in a cocktail shaker.
2. Shake and strain into a chilled cocktail glass.
3. Garnish with the lemon twist.

ACCESSORIES TO THE CRIME

Garnishes—or, in proper plural French, *garnitures*—tend to be paid little attention in today's cocktail-deprived culture. Which is a shame, because good drink garnishes, like the best floral arrangements, can add a visual thrill as well as a distinctive bouquet when properly prepped and applied.

Okay, let's not get carried away. We're not talking orchids, here; we're talking, for the most part, about citrus twists. How does one turn a mere lemon, lime, or orange rind into a fragrant spiral that can catapult a mixed drink into the heady category of classic cocktail?

Here's how:

1. Buy the ripest, brightest, firmest fruits you can find, without a whisper of green on their rinds.

2. Get yourself an ultrasharp vegetable peeler. Peelers are so inexpensive that, if you haven't replaced yours for the past year or more, it may be worth investing in a new one.

3. Cradle the fruit in your weaker hand. With your stronger hand,

draw the peeler across the surface of the fruit to a depth that just touches the whitish pulp of the fruit's subterranean skin, yet does not invade its tiny sacks of juice just below.

4. If all goes well you should be left with strips, an inch or so in length, of lemon, lime, and/or orange peel. Let them rest in cool water until they're called into service. Then twist the chosen strip in opposite directions from each end so that its fragrant oils may be released, and drop it into the cocktail for which it is destined.

Other garnishes, such as maraschino cherries, cocktail onions, and celery stalks, are low-maintenance and self-explanatory. It should be noted, however, that the best cocktail olives—those knowing green eyes that stare at us from the depths of martinis—should be small and completely devoid of pimentos.

NONALCOHOLIC COCKTAILS

Nondrinkers should be given special attention at every party. This rule is especially important on New Year's Eve, when so many festivities are centered on drinking, bubbly in particular. It's not enough to have sodas, seltzers, and juices on hand; you should also offer at least one nonalcoholic concoction that is as fun as your house cocktail and as festive as any glass of sparkling wine. Some suggestions:

• **ITALIAN SODAS.** When Italian syrup and plain seltzer are mixed together, the result is a refreshing Italian soda. Bottles of syrup are available in a wide variety of flavors—including almond, raspberry, and peppermint—at Italian specialty stores. Any kind of sparkling water will make a soda, but it's much more exciting when the seltzer comes from an old-fashioned squirter with a high-charged trigger (that onetime comedic staple technically known as a siphon bottle).

- **MICKEY MIMOSA.** Like the classic mimosa, this one's made with orange juice and bubbly. The "bubbly," however, is sparkling white grape juice. Serve it in a chilled champagne flute.
- **BABY BELLINI.** Regular Bellinis are a mix of champagne and peaches; nonalcoholic Bellinis are made with chilled sparkling cider, peach nectar, and lemon juice. Beautiful and not at all deadly.

HOT POTIONS

Ciders, mulled wines, or hot toddies—with or without alcohol—can be prepared in large batches and kept simmering in a pot on the stove during the course of your party. These bewitching brews not only warm chilled guests and tickle nondrinkers' palates, they also make your house smell divine.

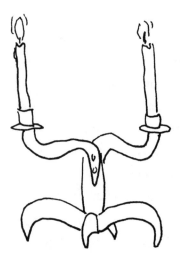

Bon Temps Toddy

(Serves about 20)

> 8 tea bags or equivalent in loose tea (try black tea, orange tea, or
> Constant Comment tea)
> 2 cups honey (or more to taste)
> 1 cup fresh lemon juice
> ¼ cup whole cloves
> 3 tablespoons ground cinnamon
> 2 tablespoons freshly grated or ground nutmeg
> 2 lemons, sliced into slim rings
> 20 cinnamon sticks, as garnish
> Bourbon, brandy, or dark rum (optional)

1. Bring 14 cups water to boil in a large stockpot or cauldron.
2. Add the tea and steep for approximately 8 minutes, then remove.
3. Add the honey, lemon juice, cloves, cinnamon, and nutmeg. Simmer over low heat for approximately 10 minutes, then adjust the seasonings as desired.
4. Float the lemon slices in the mixture. Simmer on lowest stove setting.
5. Serve in mugs or punch cups with cinnamon sticks as garnish.

TIP: Have a bottle of bourbon, brandy, or dark rum nearby and invite guests to spike their own, if desired.

Red Hot Toddy

1. Make as above, but instead of tea use cranberry juice.
2. For an extraspecial touch, add fresh cranberries to the cups before serving.

MULLED CIDER

1 gallon fresh apple cider
½ cup honey
3 tablespoons dried orange peel
3 tablespoons whole cloves
2 tablespoons cardamom seeds
2 teaspoons ground cinnamon
1 teaspoon ground nutmeg
1 teaspoon ground ginger
1 teaspoon ground allspice
18 cinnamon sticks, as garnish
Apple or ginger brandy (optional)

1. Combine the cider, honey, orange peel, cloves, cardamom seeds, cinnamon, nutmeg, ginger, and allspice in a stockpot or cauldron and warm over medium-high heat.
2. Stir until the honey is dissolved.
3. Reduce the heat and simmer about 15 minutes; adjust the flavorings as desired.
4. Serve in small cups with cinnamon sticks as garnish; offer apple or ginger brandy to add, if desired.

NEW PUNCHES FOR NOW PEOPLE

Many modern hosts and hostesses don't think of themselves as "punch people." Who can blame them? Over the years, while the rest of cuisine has evolved into new heights of enlightenment, punch has stayed back, still consisting of goofy ingredients like ginger ale and grenadine, as well as bizarre and potentially dangerous mixes of liquors.

(Riesling, rum, cherry brandy, Triple Sec, and champagne? Ouch!) Most "classic" punch recipes taste like liquid candy and pack a wallop so disabling that nobody can punch back.

But punch, properly conceived and executed, can be a party-giver's best friend. Think of what punch has going for it: (1) It's easy to make; (2) It's gorgeous; and (3) It's simple to serve (no mixing or fussing required).

There's no real mystery to punch: it's just a big cocktail in a bowl. Ah, but there's the rub: What if you don't have a punch bowl? Not to worry. Punch can be presented in almost any kind of vessel, including large salad bowls, hollowed-out watermelons, oversize metal mixing bowls, or big ol' pasta pots. Nestled in a wreath of fresh greens or in the center of a snarl of silver foil stars, even a galvanized bucket makes a fine punch bowl.

FUZZY PARTY PUNCH
(SERVES 12)

This variation on the mimosa has, at its heart, a decorative block of ice in which orange and lime slices swirl.

FOR THE ICE BLOCK:
2 oranges or blood oranges, sliced thin
1 lime, sliced thin

FOR THE PUNCH:
1 12-ounce can of frozen orange juice concentrate
2 cups orange- or lemon-flavored seltzer (unsweetened)
2 bottles champagne or sparkling wine
Lemon rind curls, for garnish

TO MAKE THE ICE BLOCK:

1. Saw the top off a clean one-gallon milk carton (or similar vessel).
2. Fill about one-third of the container with water. Add slices of 1 orange or blood orange, and freeze until solid.
3. Fill the container by another third with water. Add slices of lime, and freeze solid.
4. Fill the last third of the container with water, and add remaining orange or blood orange slices. Leave about one inch of space at the top, and freeze until solid. When you're ready to serve the punch, use scissors to cut the carton open and remove the ice block.

TO MAKE THE PUNCH:

1. Pour the frozen orange juice into the punch bowl.
2. Add the seltzer, and stir until the juice is dissolved.
3. Immediately before serving, place the ice block in the center of the bowl.
4. Add the champagne, and gently stir.
5. Serve in champagne flutes with lemon curls.

2,000 FLUSHES
(SERVES 20)

This is the carefree way to rinse away the old year and keep the new year fresh and clean.

1 12-ounce can frozen lemonade
1 cup lemon- or orange-flavored seltzer (unsweetened)
1 bottle (750 ml) blue curaçao
2 bottles champagne or sparkling wine
Ice block (see "Fuzzy Party Punch"; the size depends on the size of your punch bowl)
Plastic daisies, with stems removed (optional)

1. Pour the frozen lemonade, seltzer, and curaçao into a large punch bowl (a clear or white bowl works best for this one). Stir until lemonade is dissolved.
2. Immediately before serving, add the ice block.
3. Slowly add the sparkling wine, and stir gently.
4. Float plastic daisies on top of mixture.
5. Serve in punch cups.

CRANBERRY BOUNCE

(SERVES 12)

This is the simplest punch in the world, and so beautiful, it's like drinking jewelry.

2 12-ounce cans frozen condensed cranberry juice cocktail
3 cups vodka
1 cup fresh cranberries
½ cup Rose's Lime Juice
Juice of 2 lemons, freshly squeezed
Ice cubes
1 lime, sliced into rings

1. Pour the frozen cranberry juice into a large punch bowl.
2. Add vodka and stir until dissolved.
3. Add cranberries, Rose's Lime Juice, lemon juice, and as much ice as possible; stir gently.
4. Float the lime slices on top.
5. Serve in punch cups or wineglasses.

GOOD MEASURES

When mixing cocktails, it helps to know the capacity of various glassware; ponies and jiggers can themselves be used as measures.

Pony = 1 ounce
Jigger = 1 $\frac{1}{2}$ ounces
Cocktail Glass = 2 to 3 $\frac{1}{2}$ ounces
Highball Glass = 8 ounces
Collins Glass = 10 or 12 ounces
Zombie Glass = 12 ounces or more

BARKEEPING SECRETS

* "Up" means chilled, but served without ice. "On the rocks" means served over ice. "Neat" means no ice, served at room temperature.

* Clear liquors (like vodka, gin, and rum) should always be served as cold as possible. Brandies and cognacs should be kept at room temperature. Whiskeys, including Scotch, bourbon, and rye, can go either way, but mixed drinks, no matter what liquors they contain, are almost always served cold, sometimes on ice.

* Cocktails like martinis and Manhattans that contain only (or mostly) liquor should be stirred vigorously with a long bar spoon (a chopstick will do in a pinch), then strained into chilled stemmed glasses. The stem keeps the cocktail away from warm hands.

* Cocktails made with fruit juices, milk, or cream should be shaken, then strained. Once again, stemware should be employed.

* Vodka can replace gin in almost any cocktail recipe.

CARAVAGGIO PUNCH

(SERVES 12)

This punch gets its name because the bright fruit floating in the dark liquid looks like a painting by Caravaggio. Since it's inspired by Spanish sangria, you may prefer to call it Picasso Punch; either way, it's very artistic.

> 1 cup Constant Comment tea, strongly brewed with 2 bags or
>   equivalent in loose tea
> 3 tablespoons sugar
> 1 orange, sliced
> 1 lime, sliced
> 1 cup green seedless grapes, halved
> 1 cup red seedless grapes, halved
> 2 bottles dry red wine (preferably Spanish Rioja)
> 2 starfruits, sliced

1. Brew tea, add sugar, and let cool.
2. In a large pitcher, combine the orange and lime slices and the grapes. Add tea and one bottle of red wine. Chill for at least 2 hours or overnight.
3. Pour the chilled mixture into the punch bowl, then add the remaining wine to fill. Stir gently.
4. Float the starfruits on top.
5. Serve in wineglasses or punch cups without ice.

NOTE: Over ice in tall glasses this makes a refreshing summer punch.

FOUR...

An Effervescent Education

*C*hampagne—also known as sparkling wine, depending on where it's from—is so much a part of New Year's Eve that one can barely imagine celebrating the holiday without it. It would be like Thanksgiving without turkey, a birthday without cake, the Fourth of July without fireworks.

Yet sparkling wine, for all its popularity in our country, is something of a mystery to many Americans.

Like gourmet cuisine, fine cigars, and haute couture, good sparkling wine is born of passion. It is lovingly crafted from grape varieties that have been constantly perfected over hundreds of years. To create the clean taste and the invigorating sparkle that tickles our noses, vintners must combine the *yang* of fresh fruits from brand-new harvests with the *yin* of aged wines from former crops. It's a painstaking process that happens one batch at a time, carried out by skilled artisans who answer only to history, tradition, and a standard of quality so high-pitched that only certain people can hear it.

Truman Capote, in an effort to describe the sensuousness of sparkling wine, once wrote of its "pale blaze, a chilled fire of such prickly dryness that, swallowed, seems not to have been swallowed at all, but instead to have been turned to vapors on the tongue, and burned there to one sweet ash." Winston Churchill was more interested in its aftereffects: "A single glass of champagne," he wrote, "imparts a feeling of exhilaration. The nerves are braced; the imagination is stirred; the wits become more nimble."

The truth of sparkling wine is in the drinking of it. And like art and music, the more you know about it, the better it can be appreciated, savored, and cherished.

THE BIRTH OF THE BUBBLY

Dom Pérignon, the seventeenth-century cellarmaster of the Abbey of Hautvillers, is credited with the invention—or at least the refinement—of what we have come to know as champagne. (In his day it was called *vin saute bouchon,* "the wine with the jumping cork.") Legend has it that, while sampling the results of his first successful bottle, the blind monk shouted to his brethren, "Come quickly, I am drinking stars!"

True champagne comes from France and is, like much of French culture, subject to strict laws. It must be made from a high-quality blend of grapes (usually pinot noir, chardonnay, pinot blanc, or pinot meunier); these must be grown and harvested in the Champagne region, east of Paris; and the blend must be bottle-fermented in a hundred-step process known as *méthode champenoise.*

Méthode champenoise is used all over the world to produce sparkling wines. The Spanish version of champagne is called *cava.* Italians know it as *spumante,* in Germany it's called *Sekt,* and in other regions of France it's known as *vin mousseux.* American vintners tend to be less formal about what is or isn't champagne and can create sparkling wine from a broader variety of grapes.

DRY, DRIER, DRIEST

Labels on bottles of champagne and sparkling wine hold all kinds of important, sometimes intriguing, information. First and foremost is each wine's degree of dryness, which is determined by how much sugar is added during processing.

• The very driest sparkling wines are called *brut* and contain as little as 1 percent and no more than 1.5 percent sugar. Brut varieties are especially popular in the United States, where dryness is perceived as an indicator of quality; this is probably because inferior domestic sparkling wines are sometimes loaded with sugar.

• Slightly less dry are the *extra-dry* or *extra-sec* varieties, which are 1.2 to 2 percent sugar.

• On the sweet side are *sec* sparklers, with 1.7 to 3.5 percent sugar.

• *Demi-sec* sparkling wines are sweet enough to be considered dessert wines. They contain 3.3 to 5 percent sugar.

• The sweetest of all are *doux*, which are more than 5 percent sugar.

THE VINTAGE

Most sparkling wines that undergo the traditional *méthode champenoise* are blends of newly fermented grapes and older wines. They're mixed in careful percentages under the watchful eye of the *chef de cave,* so that every bottle is consistent with the distinctive style of the winery, known in sparkling wine lingo as the "house." Because they contain both older and newer grapes, these bottles are considered nonvintage and are usually the house's biggest yield and best value.

Occasionally a particular harvest is almost too good to be true. In those banner years grapes from a single harvest are made into champagne that's labeled "vintage." In France vintage champagnes are entirely constituted from a single year's crop; in California "vintage" means that 95 percent of the grapes are from the same outstanding year. Houses declare their own vintage years, so a given year may be vintage for one brand and nonvintage for another.

A particularly rare type of vintage champagne is called "prestige." It represents a house's very best product. Generally made from the first pressing of outstanding grapes and aged longer than average, prestige wines are usually fermented in special-issue bottles.

THINK PINK

Pink champagne, in the eyes of certain beholders, is considered even more beautiful than its amber-colored counterpoint. Unfortunately, pink bubbly has gained a bad reputation over the years; many consumers assume that it's sweet and cheap, sort of the Shirley Temple of sparkling wines. Not true. Pink sparkling wine is a genuine rosé variety, and its enchanting hue is a natural by-product of the skins of pinot grapes.

SIZE MATTERS

It is generally agreed that the bigger the bottle, the better the sparkling wine will taste—up to a point. Over the years, champagne makers have expanded into very timid and extremely bold territories, creating ever-smaller and ever-larger bottles.

• **BENJAMIN** (187 milliliters; 2 glasses; one-quarter the size of a standard bottle). Perfect to order at a table for one, or on short airplane flights.

• **SPLIT** (375 milliliters; 3 glasses; one-half the size of a standard bottle). Recommended for first dates. If it's going well, gamble on a full-size bottle.

- **BOTTLE** (750 milliliters; 6 glasses). This is the standard size seen the world over; not too heavy nor too light, it is the perfect size gift to bring to hosts and hostesses, on New Year's Eve or anytime.
- **MAGNUM** (1.5 liters; 12 glasses; 2 standard bottles). Casually called "mag" by waiters and wine merchants. No relation to the *Magnum Force* movies.
- **JEROBOAM** (3 liters; 24 glasses; 4 standard bottles). Named after the first king of the northern kingdom of Israel, who was notorious for warlike ways and idol worshipping.
- **REHOBOAM** (4.5 liters; 36 glasses; 6 standard bottles). Named for the son of Solomon, who succeeded Jeroboam.
- **METHUSELAH** (6 liters; 48 glasses; 8 standard bottles). Named after the man who, according to the Bible, survived 969 New Year's Eves.
- **SALMANAZAR** (9 liters; 72 glasses; 12 standard bottles). The bottle of the last king of the Israelites, who ruled in about 600 B.C.
- **BALTHAZAR** (12 liters; 96 glasses; 16 standard bottles). Although champagne was not on the gift registry, this bottle is named for one of the three kings who brought offerings to the baby Jesus.
- **NEBUCHADNEZZAR** (15 liters; 120 glasses; 20 standard bottles). This bottle's namesake destroyed Jerusalem in 586 B.C., thus beginning the Babylonian captivity. Famous for his hanging gardens, he later went mad and ate grass.
- **SALOMON** (18 liters; 144 glasses; 24 standard bottles). Special-issue bottles produced in 1986 for the centennial of the Statue of

Liberty. Not to be confused with Solomon, father of Rehoboam.

• **SOVEREIGN** (27 liters; 216 glasses; 36 standard bottles). Novelty bottle created to christen ships, notably the *Sovereign of the Seas* (thus the name). Also used by Lauren Bacall to christen *Monarch of the Seas*. At that event the 77-pound bottle was not hoisted by Miss Bacall but rather suspended by a system of pulleys that allowed her to simply snip a cord.

THE AGE OF SPARKLING WINE

There are many things in this world that get better with age, including women, fine wines, and Paul Newman. But champagne does not. Sparkling wine is fermented in the bottle during a three-year process (the aforementioned *méthode champenoise*), and is usually released to the marketplace when it's ready to be uncorked and consumed. Properly stored—that is, on its side, so that the cork remains moist, and in a cool dark place—champagne can stay at its peak for six months to three years. But it's folly to put away any bottle of sparkly for some far-off occasion.

One of champagne's special charms is that it's young and ripe. An eager, vivacious wine, it tickles and teases the palate with tiny explosions. Though its body may be light, medium, or full, and its flavors may be toasty or yeasty, one of the reasons that sparkling wine is so treasured is that it lacks the worldly, wizened overtones that other wines develop while gathering dust in a dank cellar. Sparkling wine is magic, and it comes to us like a genie in a bottle, ready to be unfurled with a flourish and grant all our wishes.

TAKE A CHILL

Sparkling wine should be served very cold. Standard serving temperature is 45°F, but some connoisseurs recommend chilling it as low as 36°F—which is colder than most refrigerators. Therefore, if you have very good sparkling wine and want to treat it right, let it sit for 30 minutes in a champagne bucket (a cooler or the bathroom sink will do) filled with ice and cold water.

HOW TO OPEN A BOTTLE OF SPARKLING WINE

There are many ways to open a bottle of bubbly. The Three Stooges preferred to shoot the cork across the room, where it would ricochet off some dignitary's monocle. In stadium locker rooms champagne is not a beverage but a body wash; therefore it is always shaken up until it explodes on as many half-naked linebackers as possible. In sitcoms and romantic comedies, the champagne bottle is an important test of sophistication that must be tackled by hapless Romeos on big dates. If Mr. Wonderful can open the bottle without soaking or blinding his dream girl, he's home free. Usually the bottle wins.

In the real world there is one right way to open a bottle of sparkling wine, and it does not involve shaking, popping, shooting, spraying, or spewing. A popped champagne cork is no joke: it can fly as far as 177 feet (as proved by a Guinness record-breaker in 1988) and do some serious damage along the way. It can also waste precious bubbly, which in itself is a crime.

Here's the proper procedure:

1. Like any vessel under pressure, sparkling wine bottles are

volatile and unpredictable—that is, they can flip their lids at any time. So always keep the bottle pointed away from dignitaries, linebackers, and dates.

2. Remove the foil wrapper from the top part of the neck area.

3. While keeping the cork stabilized with one hand, untwist but don't remove the metal cage that holds the cork in place.

4. Cloak the top of the bottle with a bar cloth or hand towel.

5. Hold the top firmly, then gently twist the bottle out from under the cork. You'll know you've succeeded if, when the cork is removed, the bottle lets out nothing more dramatic than an easy sigh.

6. When it comes to pouring sparkling wine, slowness is a virtue. Tilting the glass while pouring will help keep it from foaming up and over the rim, but even that's not necessary if the bubbly is dispensed in a very slow, very steady stream.

SPARKLING STEMWARE

Sparkling wine is best served in the tall, narrow stem glasses known as flutes, tulips, or trumpets. Crystal is a better choice than glass, because the surface of crystal is naturally rougher than glass and encourages more bubbles to form. (Tricky caterers have been known to scratch up the bottoms of cheap champagne glasses so that bubbles will flow more freely.) Basically, champagne will taste wonderful, no matter what you sip it from (high heels included), but here are some distinctions among the most popular bubbly glasses:

- **FLUTE:** Narrow and straight-sided. (Baccarat crystal flutes, which sell for about $90 each, are widely regarded as the very best.)
- **TULIP:** Narrow, with a rim that curves inward.

- **TRUMPET:** Narrow, with a rim that flares outward.
- **COUPE:** Saucer-shaped, like a tiny birdbath. Generally frowned upon by those in the know.

Whether you're sipping from a Baccarat flute or a scratched-up knockoff, you should always hold your glass by the stem, in order to keep your bubbly as cool as possible. At the proper temperature and in the right stemware, champagne can keep sending up jets for 45 minutes or longer.

Note: Though it's okay to chill glasses when you're serving champagne cocktails, straight-from-the-bottle bubbly keeps its effervescence longest in cool, dry glasses.

AIN'T NO FOUNTAIN HIGH ENOUGH

The saucer-shaped glasses known as coupes are lovely to look at but have been all but banished by champagne-lovers. Why? Because the coupe's wide surface area causes sparkling wine to lose its bubbles too quickly. Also, there's a problem of balance: these glasses are so prone to tipping, sloshing, and splashing that the tiniest touch of an elbow can make even swanlike creatures look oafish.

Coupes must be used, however, if you decide to thrill your guests by pouring a champagne fountain. This is no Hollywood trick—it actually works. Here's how: Assemble 10 champagne glasses on a very level surface. Arrange six of them in a circle, making sure all rims are touching. Place three glasses in a triangular arrangement on top of the six, then top the pyramid with a single glass. Pour a magnum of sparkling wine gently and slowly into the top glass, and watch the other glasses fill.

If you have enough glasses, you can make very tall champagne fountains. One of the tallest on record was nearly 26 feet high and engaged 23,642 glasses arranged in 47 layers, or stories. But even if you stick to the more manageable 10, it's wise to practice your fountain-pouring expertise with water before you attempt to impress your assembled visitors with the real stuff.

GILDING THE LILY

Purists tend to poo-poo anything that dilutes the intensity and flavor of sparkling wine. But champagne cocktails are luscious, and can dignify any glass of sparkly that's slightly below top shelf. Some popular additives:

- a dash of Chambord (to make a Kir Royal)
- a jigger of chilled stout (to make a Black Velvet)
- a splash of dry sherry
- a touch of port
- a fresh strawberry
- a cube of sugar to which has been added a few drops of cognac, Armagnac, Pernod, or bitters (to make a Champagne Cocktail).

LEFTOVERS?

It's hard to imagine such a thing, but if you find yourself with a few half-empty bottles of bubbly, here's what to do:

- A champagne corker, available at any good wine shop, will help delay sparkling wine's rapid flattening.
- If you don't have a corker, put a silver spoon into the bottle, handle first, and let it dangle, uncovered. This mysterious trick is reported to keep sparkling wine frisky for longer than usual.

SPARKLING TRIVIA

➤ The average bottle of sparkling wine or champagne has 49 million bubbles.

➤ One in ten Americans has sipped or would sip champagne from a lover's shoe.

➤ The champagne used to christen a ship is a substitute for human blood and hearkens back to the days when Vikings sacrificed people on the prows of their ships so that the spirits of the victims would guard the craft. Eventually red wine replaced blood; in eighteenth-century France the tradition of smashing champagne on new ships began.

➤ To celebrate its hundredth anniversary, Jell-O introduced a sparkling white grape flavor, touted as "The Champagne of Jell-O." Its preparation calls for two cups of seltzer or club soda.

➤ If you drop a raisin in a glass of sparkling wine, it will do a little dance. This might be because the raisin is happy to be with other former grapes.

• Flat sparkling wine is great to cook with. Scramble it into eggs; poach salmon in it; blend it with butter and herbs as a simple sauce for fish, vegetables, pasta, or grilled bread.

• If one of your New Year's resolutions is never to cook again, rinse your hair with your leftover sparkling wine. It is reputed to add blindingly beautiful shine, particularly to blond hair.

• Don't attempt to take a champagne bath. Though both Sarah Bernhardt and Marilyn Monroe are associated with the ultimate bubble bath, in truth alcohol and carbonation can irritate certain, um, delicate tissues.

THREE

That's Entertainment

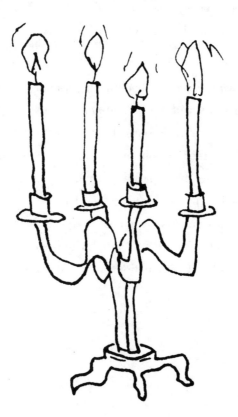

*Q*uick: What do you think of when you hear the word *entertainment*? Do you conjure up images of jugglers and tap-dancers? Do you see contortionists, ventriloquists, and fading vaudevillians spinning plates on *The Ed Sullivan Show*?

If so, you need to update your mental entertainment files.

There's an old saying in showbiz circles: "People hear with their eyes." In nonshowbiz terms, that means that a party isn't a great party unless it *looks* like a great party.

In other words, much depends on visuals.

So before you start stocking up on party hats and scouring the Yellow Pages for disk jockeys, give serious thought to decor and atmosphere. Because that, too, is entertainment.

SETTING THE STAGE:
HOW TO TRANSFORM A DREARY APARTMENT, A KID-STAINED SPLIT-LEVEL, OR A STONE-COLD CONDO INTO A PARTY PALACE

When it comes to creating enchanting ambience, three key elements do the trick: (1) lots of darkness; (2) splashes of brightness; and (3) altars.

Here's the deal:

1. Darkness is absolutely essential if a good party is going to take place. It adds mystery, erases wrinkles, disguises unsightly roots, and

makes your workaday abode look like a den of intrigue where sly, racy, and possibly dangerous things can happen.

2. Brightness is all about placement. When pools of light shine in darkened rooms, visual drama results. Imagine, for example, a corner in which everything is dim and shadowy except for a crown bearing the numerals *2000,* glittering in a hot circle of blazing whiteness. You barely need any other decorations.

3. Altars are not necessarily religious shrines. On New Year's Eve they might be display areas in which everything has been lovingly arranged for maximum eye appeal. All food areas, from buffets to dessert carts to hors d'oeuvre trays, should look like sumptuous offerings to some goddess of abundance. In each room there should be at least one table, mantelpiece, or credenza festooned with flowers, candles, baubles, and props against which guests can enact their best millennial memories.

CUNNING LIGHTING TRICKS

• Use nothing but candles to light your party. Cluster tall candles on high surfaces (mantels and the like), and place short votive candles in glass holders on low surfaces. Be careful not to put candles in any area where they might come in contact with hairdos, sleeves, or pouf skirts, and make sure your smoke alarm is in working order. Note: Avoid scented candles, as they will detract from the flavor and aroma of food and can become overwhelming in quantity.

• Replace regular lightbulbs with colored lightbulbs. You can mix these up so that each room has contrasting pools of color, or you can divide them so your guests can enjoy the Amber Room, the Red Room, or the Blue Room.

• Have fun with Christmas lights. Choose either multicolored or single-color strands, and drape them in clusters across the ceilings, or wrap furniture, sculptures, and house plants with them. Use them to frame every window and wall in your home, or bunch them together and set them out in glowing bowls.

• Borrow a slide projector and project shapes onto the walls and ceilings. You can do this by making an acetate stencil and sandwiching it into a slide frame.

• Rent a mirror ball and keep a pin spot on it all night.

MUSIC MAKES THE MILLENNIUM

Without music, a party isn't a party. It might be an assembly, a meeting, or a bee, but it can never be a shindig, a bust-up, or a ball unless there's fine tunes that never stop.

There are a number of ways to set your New Year's Eve to music. The easiest is to borrow the best stereo system you can find with a multi-CD changer in it. Prearrange groups of CDs for each anticipated phase of the evening, then you'll only have to refill the CD player in groups, and set it on "shuffle"—instant deejay.

When choosing your soundtrack, remember that music choreographs your guests. Set one should be conversation music; set two should be somewhat livelier and sexier; set three should be all-out party tunes that inspire outbursts of spontaneous dancing.

IT'S ALIVE!

Of course, you can also hire a band. (Warning: Musicians charge their highest rates on New Year's Eve.) For this you'll need lots of space,

A PARTY DISK MIX
Set One

Various artists, *Cocktail Hour* (SONY MUSICAL MEALS)
Squirrel Nut Zippers, *The Inevitable Squirrel Nut Zippers* (MAMMOTH)
Various artists, *The Crime Scene: Spies, Thighs & Private Eyes* (CAPITOL ULTRA LOUNGE)
Esquivel, *Cabaret Mañana* (RCA)
Bobby Darin, *The Best of Bobby Darin* (CAPITOL)

Set Two

Tom Jones, *Greatest Hits* (LONDON)
Etta James, *Tell Mama* (CHESS)
Donald Fagen, *The Nightfly* (WARNER BROS.)
Gipsy Kings, *Gipsy Kings* (ELEKTRA)
Taj Mahal, *Dancing the Blues* (PRIVATE MUSIC)

Set Three

Various artists, *Pure Party* (RHINO)
The O'Jays, *Love Train: The Best of the O'Jays* (LEGACY)
Tito Puente, *El Rey del Timbale* (RHINO)
Sly and the Family Stone, *Greatest Hits* (EPIC)
Al Green, *Greatest Hits Volume II* (MOTOWN)

LIVE ENTERTAINMENT
Do's and Dont's

- **Do** hire an Elvis impersonator
- **Don't** hire an introspective singer-songwriter with an acoustic guitar
- **Do** hire a large R&B band with a horn section • **Don't** hire your kid brother's garage band
- **Do** hire a salsa band • **Don't** hire a Grateful Dead tribute band
- **Do** hire an African drumming band • **Don't** hire a Dixieland band
- **Do** hire a mariachi band • **Don't** hire a lone cellist
- **Do** hire a kickin' deejay • **Don't** hire an uncooperative deejay

plenty of power, good acoustics, and very forgiving neighbors.

Live music can make or break a party. Bands don't necessarily need stages or tons of space, but they do need rooms with sound absorption. If they're stuck in a space with, say, a wall of windows or a very high ceiling, you might get an echoey mess with no definition. Bands, for their part, need to provide a good sound system. Otherwise your guests will be tormented by distortion, feedback, and/or music that's oppressively loud. Once those hurdles are cleared, make sure the band's repertoire isn't redundant, relentless, undanceable, or inappropriate. That, too, will empty a room.

When the music's right, however, it's very, very right. Nothing can transform a mere gathering into a swinging bash faster than a good band. Whether it's a 12-piece orchestra or a power trio, the right combo inspires its audience to shake it out, loosen up, get close, get rhythm, get happy. And a good bandleader is a great help when it's time to count down to midnight.

BEYOND BANDS

If live music isn't right for your budget, your crowd, or your space, open your mind to the wide world of performing arts. What about hiring belly dancers or a small acrobatic troupe? Would your guests like to be entertained by a roving magician or a rude clown? Since it's New Year's Eve, hiring a fortune-teller, a psychic, a palm reader, or an astrologer is a stroke of genius. He or she can set up a table behind a curtain and give readings to all your lucky guests, one at a time.

Also consider "piano bar" pianists, those nimble-fingered maestros who seem to know the words and music to every song ever written; musical novelty acts (the Ethel Merman Choir comes to mind); drag performers; and celebrity impersonators, whose arrival always blows a crowd away.

THE LOST ART OF PARTY GAMES

If you haven't played one lately, you might be surprised to find out how much fun party games can be, not just because they make you laugh till you fall off chairs. It's because of mob mentality.

Let me explain. At every truly great event, there's a moment when every individual loses his or her private ego and becomes part of a greater whole. You can see it happen at weddings, when otherwise respectable guests join conga lines and put garters on their heads. It happens at football games, when people in mufflers jump from their seats and wave goofy pennants, and at baseball games when nobody—even stick-in-the-muds—can resist doing The Wave. When everybody in a room rises and raises a glass and yells, "Mazel tov!" or when the beat on a dance floor suddenly catches fire and everyone grooves in a groove beyond their control, *that's* a good party.

Party games make such magic happen. Dullards become witty. Wallflowers get sexy. Frat boys acquire depth; stuffed shirts burst their buttons.

The games themselves have got to be appealing and appropriate, of course, otherwise no one will play them. So here are some games that will set your living room spinning, in a manner of speaking.

• **PASS THE ORANGE.** This traditionally teenage game involves a single orange and the limbs and joints of everyone you know. It starts with one person (probably you) placing an orange under his/her neck and passing it to the next person in line. There's only one rule: No hands. If the orange drops while you're passing it, you're out. The game goes on until one person—or perhaps a particularly agile couple—is left holding the antirickets device. The winner or winners earn a prize.

• **CONCUSSION.** This requires lots of advance preparation on your part. You are required to write the names of celebrities or well-known people on peel-back "Hello My Name Is" labels. Each participant's forehead is plastered with a name that he or she can't see (for example, Rosie O'Donnell, the Pillsbury Dough Boy, Dr. Kevorkian). The object is for people to guess their secret identity by asking yes-or-no questions. "Am I a cartoon?" is a good question, as is "Am I dead?" The first person to guess who they are gets a prize; last person to find out gets a booby prize.

- **CHARADES.** Totally corny. Really fun. Charades takes on a delicious twist if you eschew traditional categories like "movies" or "books," and instead act out categories like "junk foods," "pop icons," or "drugs."

- **PICTIONARY CHARADES.** This is played with a standard Pictionary game, but instead of drawing clues, game-players act them out. "Jogging" is easy; "adultery" is more of a challenge. Note: No props are allowed, but standard Charades signals—"sounds like," "rhymes with," and so on—are perfectly legal.

- **BINGO.** Don't knock Bingo till you've tried it. Millions of blue-haired ladies can't be wrong—after all, they managed to have fun all through Prohibition. Bingo is a great group game because everybody plays all at once. Buy a standard Bingo game, and make up your own version—for instance, you have to form the letter T on your card, or you must make the shape of a martini glass, or you have to get one chip in each corner—and have fabulous prizes or plenty of anted-up cash on hand to reward the winners.

TWO

Midnight in Your Very Own Garden of Good and Evil

*C*reating a countdown worthy of the year 2000 might be the biggest party challenge to come around in, well, 1,000 years. It simply won't be enough to cheer and kiss a few pals; people are going to want to bust out into the streets, watch the ball drop, log on to the Internet, watch fireworks, call their mother, and dive naked into the Pacific Ocean, all at once.

In other words everyone will want to feel like part of a global celebration.

What's a host/hostess to do? If you're lucky enough to have a home theater system or a wide-screen TV, that will certainly come in handy, since the party in Times Square is based upon mammoth video images that will be broadcast live as the millennium dawns all over the world. (The show begins at 7 A.M. on December 31 and continues for 24 hours.)

Moving your party at midnight to a nearby beach, field, yard, or even rooftop is a great idea; fireworks displays are scheduled just about everywhere, and nothing makes a person feel more like a child of the planet than oohing and aahing while bombs burst in air. Parties on boats will be extraspecial for this reason, as hundreds of craft blast their horns at a lit-up sky, joining the song of the universe.

If you do have your own piece of land, plan on building a millennial bonfire. This can be fed with symbolic fuel. Pieces of paper with bad years written on them, names of people, places, and things that you'd like to forget, bad habits you'd like to lose, and curses you'd like to see lifted can all be thrown into the flames. Letters to the future, letters to the past; wishes, prayers, effigies, and messages of love; these can all be thrown into the fire so that their energy will be released into the invisible world and travel to their intended destinations. (Bonfires are, in some cultures, built in order to reach the gods and communicate with the dead.)

Some other creative ways to celebrate midnight:

• Invite your guests to bring objects to be buried in a time capsule; lower it into the ground, and toss flowers in after it.

• Hand out outrageous fortune cookies with personalized predictions for the millennium.

• Get bearded and mustachioed guests to line up and shave off their whiskers.

• Hire a tattoo artist to create tiny "2000" tattoos on the bodies of gutsy guests.

• Hook up one or more speaker phones, and share the moment with other parties.

• Rent a bubble machine and fill the room with bubbles.

• Have a mystery guest jump out of a cake.

• Ask guests to announce their New Year's resolutions on videotape. Next year, show the tape as *America's Phoniest Home Videos.*

• Pour the tallest champagne fountain you can manage.

SHOULD AULD ACQUAINTANCE BE FORGOT?

Robert Burns is great as far as Scottish poetry goes, but he did make one false move: He wrote down the words to "Auld Lang Syne" after hearing an old man singing the traditional ballad.

Now this mournful dirge, which is almost as mournful and dirgy as "Happy Birthday to You" but with lyrics that are meaningless to 99 percent of Americans, is the song with which we welcome the New Year. We blithely sing about taking a "right guid willie-waught" and being a "pint stowpt" without having any idea what we're crooning about.

THE COMPLETE "AULD LANG SYNE"

Should auld acquaintance be forgot,
And never brought to min',
Should auld acquaintance be forgot
And days of auld lang syne.
For auld lang syne, my dear,
For auld lang syne,
We'll tak' a cup o' kindness yet,
For auld lang syne.

And here's a hand, my trusty fierce,
And gie's a hand o' thine,
And we'll tak' a right guid willie-waught,
For auld lang syne, my dear,

For auld lang syne,
We'll tak' a cup o' kindness yet,
For auld lang syne.

And surely ye'll be your pint stowpt,
And surely i'll be mine,
And we'll tak' a cup of kindness yet,
For auld lang syne.
For auld lang syne, my dear,
For auld lang syne,
We'll tak' a cup o' kindness yet,
For auld lang syne.

Though you may not be able to change the "Auld Lang Syne" tradition for good, you can, if you want, banish it from your millennial celebration. Replace it with something like "Strangers in the Night." The tune is romantic and mysterious, like New Year's Eve itself, and a surprising number of people know all the lyrics. Even if you stumble

NEW YEAR'S EVE PROPS

New Year's Eve just wouldn't be New Year's Eve without hats and horns.
But for the party of the millennium, the props need to be louder,
livelier, and more imaginative.

Try:

• Sparklers • Cowbells • Flash paper • Gongs • Canned marine horns
Metal wind chimes • Bullhorns • Flares • Kazoos • Metal whistles • Drums •
Sliding whistles • Bongos • Duck calls • Congas • Popguns • Trumpets
and saxophones • Cap guns rented for the occasion • Maracas •
Firecrackers • Tambourines • Paper poppers • Crackers • Pans and buckets
(beaten with wooden spoons)

Instead of paper hats, hand out:

• Wigs • Fedoras • Fezzes • Mardi Gras beads • Dunce caps • Play money
Propeller beanies • Top hats • Devil horns • Nose and glasses disguises •
Angel haloes • Arrows-through-heads • Feather boas • Eye patches •
Jeweled turbans • Wax lips

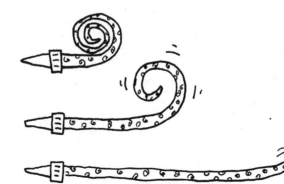

on a chorus or two, there's that friendly "doo be doo be doo" which can be understood by all peoples of all languages, and which prompts thoughts of "to be or not to be," and "to do is to be," and "do be a Do Bee," all appropriate musings for the dawn of the millennium, or any year.

There are plenty of other choices, too. Gloria Gaynor's "I Will Survive" is devilishly difficult to sing, but has a stirring, anthemlike feel. A novelty tune like "Enjoy Yourself, It's Later Than You Think" might also work, if your friends know it; "Is That All There Is" could be interesting, as could "Love Train," "Oh, Happy Day," and "In the Still of the Night." Think about passing out printouts of the lyrics to your guests to help things along.

Note: By the time you read this, Prince's "1999" will probably be so overplayed that you'll never want to hear it again as long as you live, but it might be an irresistible choice to blast over your system at the point of no return.

ONE

A Toast to the New Year

*W*herever you go and whatever you do on the midnight of the millennium, a group toast will be a highlight and a hallmark of the event.

The tradition of toasting is as old as written history. Ulysses drank to the health of Achilles. Early Greeks routinely raised their glasses to Hermes, the Graces, and Zeus. Ancient Egyptians, Persians, Hebrews, and Saxons all toasted; Attila the Hun led at least three for each course at a feast.

In seventeenth-century British society, toasting became so popular that it was considered uncivil to take a drink without toasting to some-one's health. Was it just an excuse to drink more? Maybe: Temperance societies rose up and banished toasting altogether, claiming it was the work of the devil. (To this day, Jehovah's Witnesses do not toast.)

Full-blown toasts are still de rigueur at weddings, political din-ners, and diplomatic events. But for less formal affairs, glasses are usually raised to a short blessing, a quick witticism, or a brief, amus-ing story. Toasts are tossed off, so to speak; they're little more than some variation of "down the hatch."

But the millennial toast warrants a fuss. It is an opportunity to mark a once-in-a-lifetime event and should be a scheduled part of your New Year's Eve festivities, right along with the games and the grub. The best time to stage a toast is in that small pocket of time when all your guests are gathered together and waiting for the midnight countdown to begin.

SAYING A FEW WORDS

When the smiling throngs are assembled, looking gorgeous and raising sparkling stemware in your direction, what will you say? Maybe nothing. If you're lucky enough to have someone in your crowd who is a talented speechmaker, assign the millennial toast to that person (well in advance), and let his or her words shine into the new year.

THIRTY-ONE WAYS TO SAY "CHEERS"

VIRTUALLY EVERY CULTURE HAS A CUSTOMARY BLESSING OR TOAST THAT'S JUBILANTLY SHOUTED OR REVERENTLY MURMURED EVERY TIME A GLASS IS RAISED. SOME OF THESE HAVE PECULIAR ORIGINS; THE TOAST SKÅL, OR SKOAL, FOR EXAMPLE, COMES FROM THE ANCIENT NORSE CUSTOM OF DRINKING FROM THE SKULL OF A SLAIN ENEMY. AHEM.

- ALBANIAN: GËZUAR
- ARABIC: BISMILLAH
- ARMENIAN: GENATZT
- AUSTRIAN: PROSIT
- BELGIAN FLEMISH: OP UW GEZONHEID
- BRAZILIAN PORTUGUESE: SAÚDE
- CHINESE: NIEN NIEN NU E
- DANISH/SWEDISH/NORWEGIAN: SKÅL
- DUTCH: PROOST
- EGYPTIAN: FEE SIHETAK
- FINNISH: KIPPIS
- FRENCH: A VOTRE SANTÉ
- GERMAN: PROSIT
- GREEK: EIS IGIAN
- INDIAN: JAIKING
- INDONESIAN: SELAMAT
- IRANIAN: BESALMATI
- ITALIAN: ALLA SALUTE
- JAPANESE: KAMPAI
- KOREAN: KON GANG UL WI HA YO
- PAKISTANI: SANDA BASHI
- POLISH: NA ZDROWIE
- PORTUGUESE: A SUA SAÚDE
- ROMANIAN: NOROC
- SPANISH: SALUD
- THAI: SAWASDI
- TURKISH: SEREFE
- UKRAINIAN: BOOVATJE ZDOROVI
- WELSH: IECHYD DA
- YUGOSLAVIAN SERBO-CROAT: ZIVIO
- ZULU: OOGY WAWA

SOME CLASSIC TOASTS

Ring out, wild bells, to the wild, wild sky . . .
The year is dying in the night . . .
Ring out, wild bells, and let him die.
Ring out the old, ring in the new . . .
Ring out the false, ring in the true.
—ALFRED LORD TENNYSON

May you live all the days of your lives.
—JONATHAN SWIFT

May all your troubles during the coming year
be as short as your New Year's resolutions.
—ANONYMOUS

A toast to the cocktail party, where olives are
speared and friends are stabbed.
—ANONYMOUS

Here's to a clear conscience—or a poor
memory.
—ANONYMOUS

Never do anything standing that you can do
sitting, or anything sitting that you can do
lying down.
—CHINESE PROVERB

What a piece of work is (host/hostess's name
here).
—WILLIAM SHAKESPEARE

Don't let sorrow come higher than your knees.
—SWEDISH PROVERB

I'd rather have a bottle in front of me than a
frontal lobotomy.
—TOM WAITS

I'd rather be with all of you than with the
finest people in the world.
—ANONYMOUS

When you have only two pennies left in the
world, buy a loaf of bread with one, and a lily
with the other.
—CHINESE PROVERB

To Da Vinci's notebooks; to Einstein's preoccu-
pations; to Mozart and to Bach, and to the
child who hears a canon for the first time in
"Frère Jacques"; to the singularities of chalk
and cheese and to the delectabilities of all
things, visible and invisible; I'chaim because
it is good; to health, for no reason but itself;
to men because they are men, to women without explanation, and to the good company of
every secular thing in saecula saeculorum.
Toast them with their own watchword: Here's
how!
—ROBERT FARRAR CAPON

Martinis are like a woman's breasts. One isn't
enough, and three are too many.
—ANONYMOUS

It's better to spend money like there's no
tomorrow than to spend tonight like there's no
money.
—P. J. O'ROURKE

After a good dinner one can forgive anybody, even
one's own relatives.
—OSCAR WILDE

Frivolity is the species' refusal to suffer.
—JOHN LAHR

CLINK AND DRINK

IT IS SAID THAT WINE IS A TREAT FOR ALL THE SENSES. IT IS SMELLED, TOUCHED TO THE LIPS, AND TASTED—BUT FIRST, WITH THE GENTLE CHIME OF GLASSES TOUCHING IN A TOAST, IT IS HEARD.

THOUGH IT'S A TIME-HONORED CUSTOM, NOT ALL HOSTS AND HOST-ESSES APPRECIATE THE CLINKING ROUTINE, ESPECIALLY IF YOU'RE SIP-PING FROM THEIR BEST CRYSTAL. BEFORE CLINKING, WATCH YOUR HOST AND TAKE HIS LEAD. AND ALWAYS, BE GENTLE.

If not, then you'll have to be brave and write a toast. It should cover the joys and foibles of life, touch on the glories and gaffes of your friends and loved ones, and sum up the significance of all that came before and all that lies ahead. It will also have to bring a smile to all lips, a tear to each eye, and ultimately inspire wild bursts of spontaneous cheering.

Too much pressure, you say?

Then initiate rounds of toasts in which loquacious guests are invited to say a few words. If you're at a total loss when your turn comes up, it's perfectly acceptable to borrow a toast that's tried and true.

After the Drop

*Y*ou did it. You delivered yourself and your friends into the new year, the new decade, the new century, and the new millennium on a mighty cloud of joy.

All the food was eaten. Every drinking vessel in the house was used—even the Dixie cups in the bathroom. The din of conversation rose to the point where you had to shout in order to speak to the person standing next to you. People made friends. A few fell in love. Everybody danced. No one would leave. You'll never get the confetti out of the carpets.

It was a great party.

Now, like the god Janus—for whom the month of January was named—it's time not only to gloat over the past 24 hours but also to look into the future. Beyond the next few days, which will likely involve picking up squashed party hats and finding cigarette butts in your potted palms, there is the matter of the rest of your life.

And that can mean only one thing: resolutions.

UPWARD NOBILITY

Many a New Year's resolution is based on regret. This may be because it follows months of holiday indulgence, including consuming piles of candy on Halloween, feasting shamelessly at Thanksgiving, and surfing a tsunami of drinking, debauchery, and decadence at Christmas and New Year's Eve parties.

The top two deadly sins that weak-willed citizens renounce each year are gluttony and sloth. Health clubs and weight-loss programs count on this annual epidemic of self-disgust and do their heaviest recruiting in January. Various organizations have decreed January to be Diet Month, Fat-Free Living Month, National Lose Weight/Feel Great Month, Oatmeal Month, and National Prune the Fat Month.

Committing to eat more Wheaties and fewer Snickers bars certainly has merit. But the millennium calls for something beyond physical improvement, don't you think? The millennium makes a person stop and remember that just to be alive is an extraordinary privilege. Each of us had only a one-in-300-million chance of ever being conceived in the first place. Those odds are even slimmer than the chances of winning the lottery or being killed by sniper fire. Yet here we are, survivors of childhood and puberty, witnessing the end of one 1,000-year interval and the beginning of another. It's a bona fide miracle.

Poking at one's flab and swearing to spend more time on the NordicTrack just isn't dramatic enough for these amazing times. Millennial resolutions should be grand gestures of compassion and commitment. Maybe now is the perfect time to slay all the deadly sins—not just sloth and gluttony but envy, greed, lust, pride, and anger—and replace them with the seven shining virtues of courage, purity, humility, honesty, diligence, charity, and fidelity.

Just a thought.

THE FIRST DAY OF THE REST OF YOUR MILLENNIUM

New Year's Day tends to get buried in the flotsam and jetsam of holiday fallout, and that's a shame. Because New Year's Day, though regarded by many as a bonus day of rest and returning hideous Christmas presents, has a lot going for it.

It's the day when Earth begins another orbit around the sun and starts a journey that will cover nearly 583,416,000 miles in 365.2422 days. It's a national holiday in the United States, a religious holiday for some faiths, the beginning of the fiscal year for many taxpayers, and the holiday most widely celebrated around the world.

It's also the day of the Sudan's independence celebration; it's "Everyman's Birthday"; the anniversary of Paul Revere's birth (in 1735); the anniversary of the circumcision of Christ (in 0001); Ellis Island's anniversary; Haiti's independence day; St. Basil's Day; the beginning of the Western Pacific hurricane season; Bill Gates's wedding anniversary; and Ellen DeGeneres's birthday.

You may choose to spend this day in quiet reflection, centering yourself and preparing for the sobering return to workaday reality.

On the other hand, you may want to join with others in a special observance or ritual, like watching a game and drinking beer. If that's the case, here's a small sampling of events that annually take place on January 1 across the country and the world.

• **SNO'FLY.** The first kite fly of the year, held in Kalamazoo, Michigan.

• **THE HANGOVER HANDICAP RUN.** A two-mile fun run in Klamath Falls, Oregon.

THE HIGH COST
OF TOO MUCH FUN

Even people who watch their drinking can get carried away and wake up on New Year's Day with nausea, dizziness, fatigue, eye pain, muscle aches, dry mouth, and a head that feels as though an untalented carny used it for hatchet practice.

Scientists say that there's no such thing as a true cure for a hangover. There are some popular folk remedies, however, many of which do make scientific sense.

• If you know you've gone overboard, swallow two aspirin (preferably buffered) with a large glass of water *before* going to bed. Though you may still feel fuzzy in the morning, you probably won't wake up with a headache. Ibuprofen will also do in a pinch, but avoid acetaminophen (Tylenol) because it shouldn't be mixed with large quantities of alcohol.

• Try Alka-Seltzer. Remember all those Alka-Seltzer commercials in the 1970s in which people groaned about overindulging? They weren't just talking about eating, folks. Alka-Seltzer is most effective as a night-before beverage to help keep headaches at bay and settle the stomach, but it is also useful as a morning-after tonic. Here's why: Alcohol breaks down in one's system into a whole smorgasbord of toxins, many of which are acidic. The "alka" (alkaline) in Alka-Seltzer helps counterbalance that. It also contains aspirin for your head, and because it's dissolved in water, it helps battle dehydration.

• Coca-Cola and aspirin is a classic headache cure. It is also reported to work on hangovers.

• A spoonful of baking soda dissolved in a large glass of water will start you on the road to recovery. A mix of bitters and club soda is another time-honored and terrible-tasting cure. Use either potion to wash down that miracle drug, aspirin.

• Once on your feet, load up on carbs and whatever else your body is crying for. Toast, pancakes, orange juice, corned beef hash, bananas, egg foo yung, chocolate pudding, pizza, cream soda, tomato juice, hamburgers . . . soon enough your system will balance itself and you will go forth humbled and newly determined to be more cautious in the New Year.

- **THE LONDON PARADE.** Begins at noon at Westminster Bridge and marches through Trafalgar Square and Piccadilly Circus. Draws about 1 million spectators yearly.
- **THE PARIS PARADE.** Begins at 2 P.M.; covers much of Montmartre, and passes Sacré Coeur. Draws about 100,000 yearly.
- **THE SUGAR BOWL CLASSIC.** Championship football game in New Orleans, Louisiana.
- **NEW YEAR'S BLUEGRASS FESTIVAL.** A musical celebration in Jekyll Island, Georgia.
- **OUTBACK BOWL GAME.** Top college football teams compete in Tampa, Florida.
- **NEWPORT YACHT CLUB FROSTBITE FLEET RACE.** Annual race of the brave.
- **POLAR BEAR SWIM.** Annual plunge of the very brave into Lake Michigan at Sheboygan, Wisconsin.
- **BLACK NAZARENE FIESTA.** A nine-day fiesta in Manila, Philippines, honoring the district's patron saint.
- **TUFF HEDEMAN PROFESSIONAL BULL RIDERS CHALLENGE.** A national rodeo event in Kingsville, Texas.
- **THE SHANGHAI PARADE.** A tradition in Lewisbury, West Virginia.
- **THE COTTON BOWL CLASSIC.** Postseason football game in Dallas, Texas.

INDEX